Keys to the KINGDOM

Unlocking the Power of Your Faith

By Kenneth Weathersby, D.Min.

Keys to the Kingdom
Unlocking the Power of Your Faith

Copyright © 2024 by Dr. Kenneth Weathersby

The scanning, uploading, and distribution of this book without permission constitutes a theft of the author's intellectual property. If you would like permission to use material from this book (other than for review purposes), please contact the author at kweathersby57@gmail.com. Thank you for supporting the author's rights.

Scripture quotations marked CEV are taken from the Holy Bible, *Contemporary English Version*. Copyright ©1991, 1992, 1995 by American Bible Society. Used by Permission.

Scripture quotations marked NKJV are taken from the *New King James Version*. Copyright ©1982 by Thomas Nelson. Used by permission. All rights reserved.

Scripture quotations marked KJV are taken from the Holy Bible, *King James Version*. Public Domain

Unmarked Scripture quotations represent the author's paraphrase.

ISBN: 978-0-9747600-6-3

Printed in the United States

We should have no need. See, we are praying for things, but God said "Do you not realize that the Kingdom of heaven has returned? Everything you need is in heaven." That's why we don't need to seek after money because when we do what God tells us to do, everything we need will be provided.

Jesus said don't worry about what you're going to eat. Don't worry about what you're going to wear. Don't worry about where you're going to stay. Your Father knows that you need all these things." The only responsibility we have is to seek first the Kingdom of God and align our lives with His righteousness, and all these things will be added unto us. So why in the world are we worried about stuff? God is saying that everything you have He has already given it to you, but you must learn how to pull it out of heaven to put it on earth.

> *God is saying that everything you have He has already given it to you, but you must learn how to pull it out of heaven to put it on earth.*

Everything we need is a part of the Kingdom. You see, a king is known for how well his people live. Believers in Jesus Christ are in a Kingdom. We are saints, citizens of the Kingdom. We are not members of a church. God calls us sons and daughters: "But as many as received Him, to them He gave the right to become children of God, to those who believe in His name" (John 1:12, NKJV). Therefore, God's Son, our Elder Brother is the King. We are citizens of the Kingdom, and citizens don't fight.

> *We are citizens of the Kingdom, and citizens don't fight.*

Either you are citizen or you are a soldier. Soldiers have to give up their citizenship. God said that you are citizens. Which means that everything you need is provided. Who's supposed to be fighting? The angels. The angels are asking, "Why are you trying to do my job?" The church is fighting, but God said that's not the church's job. The Bible tells us in Hebrews 1:14 (NKJV), "Are they not all ministering spirits sent forth to minister for those who will inherit salvation?" Prayer gives us access to the angels. Prayer is our number one key in the Kingdom, and that's why the Kingdom is the greatest message ever preached.

When we really understand prayer, we will change the world. Jesus' disciples saw Him walk on water. They witnessed Him healing the sick, and giving sight to the blind. They were present when Jesus borrowed a young boy's lunch of two small fish and five crusts of bread and fed more than five thousand people. Yet they did not say the Savior, "Jesus, teach us how to walk on water." They didn't say, "Jesus, teach us how to say a word and make the wind stop blowing. They didn't say "Jesus, teach us how to do miracles." But one thing they did say was "Jesus, teach us how to pray."

I don't recall anywhere in the Bible that records Jesus having corporate prayer with His disciples. The Bible said Jesus would bless the food, but I don't recall Him having prayer meetings. What I do remember reading is Jesus walking to a place of solitude early in morning. While in His private space time, Jesus utilized these precious moments to commune with Father. On one occasion, after praying on the mountain alone, Jesus came down from the mountain and the only thing He had to say to a demon was "Go!", and that demon was gone. God is saying to His people, "If you want to change your city, if you want to change your state,

Contents

Dedication

Acknowledgments

Foreword, 7

The Greatest Message Ever Preached, 9

The Just Shall Live by Faith, 23
- Five P's of Living by Faith, 27

Example of a Loving Father, 38
- A Father's Love Grants Room for Mistakes, 41
- A Father Forgives, 44
- A Father Celebrates and Secures, 45

An Attitude of Gratitude, 47
- Obedience, 52

Living Abundantly, 60
- You Must Be Born Again, 63
- Meditate and Study His Precepts and Promises, 65
- Utilize the Word, 66
- Learn How to Praise Him, 68

Living by Faith in the Kingdom, 76

About the Author, 98

Dedication

This book is dedicated in loving memory of my parents, Evelyn and Joel Weathersby, and my parents in-law, Thelma and Scott Kennedy, who planted seeds of knowledge and wisdom in me, nurtured me, inspired me, and never stopped believing in me.

I also dedicate this to my wife, Belva Kennedy Weathersby, our children, Kenyeta and Breon, and our granddaughter, Kennedi Denise. They inspire me and fill my heart with joy each and every day.

Acknowledgments

I could not have accomplished the completion of this book without the help of some people I feel compelled to acknowledge. I greatly appreciate the services of the literary midwife who helped me birth this project, Olivia M. Cloud of Guardian Angel Communications Services.

I gratefully acknowledge the support of my esteemed colleagues and brothers, Pastor Michael Pigg and Pastor Lennox Zamore for their vital assistance in helping me to take this project over the finish line.

Foreword

In this book, Dr. Ken Weathersby, a well-respected seminary-trained theologian, is offering gold bars of truth graciously revealed to him by the Holy Spirit. *Keys to the Kingdom* is about a theology that was front and center in the teachings of Jesus, the apostles, and the early Church, but seems to have receded from our modern-day theology — the Gospel of the Kingdom. Dr. Weathersby shows how Jesus did not come to earth to bring a religion, but rather, a Kingdom. He asserts that the reason why many people are not coming into relationship with the Lord Jesus Christ, especially today, is because we have not invited them into a Kingdom but into a religion by which many have become disillusioned. He will show that the greatest message that you can ever hear is that God came to restore unto us the Kingdom of God.

Dr. Weathersby will show that many believers have been delivered but have not been set free. And that while we preach repentance to the lost, we also may need to repent. He masterfully demystifies repentance as a changing of the mind. Of thinking. But also, a change of mindset and attitude. He shows how God is trying to get us to go back to the mind He gave humanity in Genesis 1 and 2. And this is a mind of faith and obedience.

He explains how in a kingdom the king owns and provides everything to his citizens. Everything has already been given to us in heavenly places. But we must learn how to pull them out of heaven to earth, and the only way to do that is through faith. He discusses concepts like faith and hope and reveals the relationship between faith and difficulty. The sentiment that a faith that cannot be tested cannot be trusted reverberates in this book.

Dr. Ken demonstrates how your faith is only as strong as the trials you have already endured. You cannot have faith if you don't have hope, which is simply something that you want for the future. He will mesmerize you with his five P's for living by faith.

And just when you think he has exhausted the Kingdom gems, Dr. Weathersby will show you that the highest character of the Kingdom is the love of the Father. He will show how a Father's love anticipates and even makes room for mistakes. And with a King who is also our Father, there is no room for worry. We have freedom from cares, from fears, and even from fighting, for we are citizens, not militia.

In this book, you will learn how to praise, how to prosper, and how to procure every Kingdom blessing, especially healing. I hope you enjoy *Keys to the Kingdom*.

Reverend Lennox Zamore
Pastor and Author

The Greatest Message Ever Preached

"For our citizenship is in heaven, from which we also eagerly wait for the Savior, the Lord Jesus Christ"
~ Philippians 3:20, NKJV

I look around in our world and especially in our country today and I ask the question: What is happening that our children, our grandchildren, do not want to embrace the faith that we have. What is governing their mindset? Many of them do not want to go to church. And I think that is the problem — we're going to church, and we are not being the Church.

It seems to me that we are repeating the days of when Jesus Christ walked the earth to call followers by faith and the people made it a religion. We likewise have turned God's plan of salvation and His Kingdom into religion. Jesus never came to start a religion. Jesus never came to put Himself in the same category with Mohammed or Buddha. Jesus came to do something that we were not able to do for ourselves. He came to restore humanity to our rightful place on this earth.

In Genesis 1:26, the Bible tells us that God made us in His image and in His likeness, and he has given us dominion over the fish of the sea, the birds of the air, the cattle, all the wild animals on earth and every creeping thing. In other words, God gave us rulership on earth. Because of what happened in Genesis 3, the rebellion of man against God, the Kingdom of God and the Holy Spirit vacated us, and another ruler came into being — the ruler of darkness. And now, some 6500 years later, the Old Testament tells us about the laws and the principles of God. Through the Old Testament we are told that a King is coming. We do not understand that Jesus came as King. He came telling us to repent, for the Kingdom of heaven is near (Matthew 4:17).

> *The greatest message that you can ever hear is that God came to restore unto us the Kingdom of God.*

The greatest message that you can ever hear is that God came to restore unto us the Kingdom of God. The work of God in restoring the Kingdom of God is why we can live in the Kingdom. Now let me say a couple of things about the Kingdom. First, many of us know very little about the Kingdom. We think the church is the Kingdom. Jesus said in Matthew 16, "I will build my Church. Notice he used the word my Church, which implies there were other churches.

I don't think we understand the purpose of the Church and that is the reason why our children do not want to have anything to do with the Church, because we don't understand the purpose of the Church. The word "church" in the Bible is a political term. It was a term that meant senate, or cabinet. It was a term the Romans used Jesus was born in a kingdom — at a time when Rome was in charge. Everybody who lived in the kingdom of Rome was under the authority of Caesar and was subject to Caesar.

Living in America robs many of us of a working knowledge of Kingdoms. We live in the Republic of the United States. Our country was started because we were rebelling against the king's rule. Galatians 14 tells us that in the fullness of time God sent His Son. Why did God send His Son in a Kingdom context? The Egyptians had already lived. The Assyrians, a great empire, had already lived. The Persians had already lived. The Babylonians, the Greeks, and all the rest of them, when they were going into a city to capture it, they would burn it down and enslave the townspeople. But Rome did not do that, being influenced by the great Greeks.

Recognize that most of what we understand today is based on Greek theology. According to Greek thought, if you didn't have blue eyes and white hair, they considered you a slave. Plato, Aristotle, Socrates are the great philosophers that we studied in college; yet we don't understand the damage it has done to our psyche. Most of us have been trained and taught by European leaders and we don't understand anything about Kingdom philosophy. Because when you understand Kingdom and the context of what Jesus came and has done for us, you would be liberated.

Many of us have been delivered, but we have not been set free.

Many of us have been delivered, but we have not been set free. When the Children of Israel were in bondage, they were in Egypt. They were delivered from Pharaoh, but God walked them around in circles for 40 years because Egypt was still in them. They were delivered, but they were not free. Then God had to allow an entire generation to die. He had to get what was in their the next generation to go into the Promised Land. Many of us are like the Hebrew children of the days of Moses; we've been delivered, but we're not set free. Only the truth will set you free.

God is calling out His Church, "the *ekklesia*" — the Greek word meaning church. *Ekklesia* is a political word used to designate an assembly of citizens of ancient Greek states. Jesus set up a government because Jesus came to take over the world. Isaiah 9:6 (KJV) reads: "For unto us a child is born, unto us a son is given: and the government shall be upon his shoulder: and his name shall be called Wonderful, Counsellor, The mighty God, The everlasting Father, The Prince of Peace."

The Bible says that the government will be upon His shoulders. So, in other words, God came to take over. He came for us to be a part of his cabinet. He was saying, "As I build my church, you are being called out to be a part of my senate. You are being called out to do what I tell you to do because I am the King." We know how a monarchy functions. Don't do what the king tells you to do and see what happens. You probably won't be around much longer. So, Jesus said, "Don't call me 'Lord, Lord,' if you won't do what I tell you to do."

Jesus was telling His disciples, "Upon this rock, upon this statement that I am the Messiah, upon this statement that I am the King, I will start my cabinet, my government. I will call you out to be part of my plan to redeem the world. No need to stress about success, the gates of Hades shall not prevail against you." The King James translation uses hell for Hades in this verse. There are three words in the Bible to describe hell — Hades, Sheol (the Old Testament word designating the abode of the dead)," and Gehenna (the word used in the New Testament to describe the dwelling place of the damned in the afterlife). Hades means the grave. Jesus was saying, "Do you not realize that the grave won't be able to prevail against My Church? I have given you the keys of the Kingdom."

Most of us do not use the keys. Many of us are just happy to be in the church, just happy to be in the house, and yet God has given you some keys that are not being utilized. Jesus calls us to repentance. You know what repent means? Repent doesn't mean to come down the aisle of your church, grab the pastor by the hand and start crying. If you go to a courtroom and stand before a judge and start crying, the judge will simply say, "We'll take a recess for five minutes to allow you to compose yourself."

Repentance means you must change your thinking.

Repentance means you must change your thinking. You must change the way you think — your attitude and your mind — to repent. Notice Jesus did not join the Pharisaic party. Nor did He did join the Sadducees. He did not join the Herodian party. He did not join the Essenes. As a matter of fact, it was the religious leaders who killed Jesus. The Bible says that the publicans, the tax collectors, and the sinners loved Him. It appears that unchurched folks loved Jesus because He did not judge them. Persons in the church have a tendency to judge other persons. Nevertheless, Jesus told us not to judge because the same way we judge would be the way that we would be judged.

Jesus tells us we must change our thinking about the Kingdom because we have been given authority. Jesus had to come to earth as a man because otherwise He would have been illegal. He had to come in a body. Human beings are, first and foremost, spirit. Each one of us is housed in a dirt suit. You got two types of dirt suits. The first was the one man, and that was Adam. The second man was Jesus. Everybody else came out of the first man, but the man came into models. Everybody's a man. You got a woman, a man with a womb. We are all one. And we must worship Him in spirit and in truth because we are a body.

For you to do what God has called you to do, you have to be living on earth. Nevertheless, we have created the theology of heaven. When you die, yes, you're going to heaven. To be absent from the body, to be present with the Lord (2 Corinthians 5:6), but God wants you to stay on earth because you have dominion on earth. John Wesley said, "Man cannot do anything without God." Then he added "But God will not do anything without man on earth." You know why? Because God loves you too much to disagree with His word. He said that he has given you dominion because he gave man dominion, but man lost the power to carry out the dominion. So now the greatest message to all humankind to hear is that the Kingdom of Heaven has returned. Now you have the power and the accessibility to allow God to do what He wants to do through you.

The reason why our world is in the shape that it's in is because we don't understand our assignment. He has given us the keys. He has given us the ability to bind some stuff on earth. He has given us the ability to open up some stuff on earth. The only thing we have to do is to allow God to use us. That's why Jesus tells us not to worry about anything.

if you want to change the world, you have to learn how to pray because you have the capacity to pull down the power of heaven to earth.

Jesus did not preach on being born again. Jesus preached on one message. He taught one man who came to him at night (see John 3). Nicodemus had heard this young preacher talking about the Kingdom of God. He came in the middle of the night, under the cover of darkness. The first thing Jesus told him was, "Unless you are born again you cannot even see the Kingdom of God. Nicodemus did not understand what Jesus was saying. Jesus said, "Unless you are born of the water and of the Spirit, you will not enter the Kingdom of God." In other words, Jesus was saying, "You must have a body and you have to be born by the Holy Spirit. And after you have done that, you are part of the Kingdom."

You can be a part of a church, but yet not be a part of the Kingdom.

You can be a part of a church, but yet not be a part of the Kingdom. That's why Jesus tells us we must learn how to pray. First, you must acknowledge the Father. The name *Abba Patēr* means Source and Sustainer. He is "Our Heavenly Father — our creator and sustainer. Therefore, you always go to God as Father, "Our Father who is in heaven." Then Jesus said you must acknowledge His majesty, "Hallowed or holy be Thy name." Then He said, "Thy Kingdom come on earth," and His will be done and made. That means His intention for His purpose. God's purpose has never changed since Genesis 1 that you and I have rulership on earth. Because of the failure of man by sinning, His plan had to change. The purpose of God is still the same.

For that reason, I think we need to start learning more about the Kingdom. We're not studying the Kingdom and all Jesus taught us about the Kingdom. The Kingdom of heaven is like this woman who went before an unjust judge…The Kingdom of heaven is like you going sow seed, and the seed is the word about the Kingdom of God… Unless you accept the Kingdom as a little child, you will not enter. That's what Jesus talked about, and the reason why that was important is because that's what we lost. We lost the Holy Spirit.

The greatest message about the Kingdom is that the Kingdom is here and everything you need is in the Kingdom. Peace is in the Kingdom. Love is in the Kingdom. Forgiveness is in the Kingdom. Everything you need comes out of the Kingdom. He says, "seek first the Kingdom of God," and then you're supposed to align your life with His righteousness. And when you align your life with Him, you have access to the supplies of the Kingdom. When you are under the King, you are His ambassador.

As an ambassador, you represent the King every second of your life.

As an ambassador, you represent the King every second of your life. Your life is not your own, you carry out the assignment of the King. So that means if someone asks you what you think about homosexuality, all you need to respond is, "Well, let me tell you what the Constitution says, the laws I live under and the principles that govern my life."

The Word of God is your constitution as you are part of His Kingdom. You are an ambassador. An ambassador doesn't have the right to say what's on his or her mind.

The ambassador only says what the government says. The ambassador will say, "My government say it is an abomination." I don't have to worry about what I think. It's not about what I think. What does the government say?

You are the children of the King. You are citizens of the Kingdom. You are ambassadors for the Kingdom. An ambassador only says what the King says. You don't have a right to say what you think. You have to say what the King says. And when you say what the King says, you are preaching the greatest message of all times — that the Kingdom of heaven has returned.

And that's why everything starts with "re." Redeem: means He owns you again. Restore: means He has put you back in the right place. Receive: the Holy Spirit, which means to have again. Reconciliation: being made one with Him again. Return: going back to where you have fallen. Everything God does is takes us back to the beginning. The Church was at the beginning with Adam and Eve and everything God does for us takes us back to the beginning. That's why it is the greatest message.

The Holy Spirit never lived with man after he lost it in the garden.

The Holy Spirit never lived with man after he lost it in the garden. The Bible said the Holy Spirit would come upon Elijah. The Holy Spirit will come upon Samuel. The Holy Spirit could not live in your temple because you were unclean. But one Friday when the King of the Jews came, and they took him to the old rugged cross. They broke his skin. That's why you are healed because they broke His skin, and the blood came out. And His blood cleanses us from all sin. Blood had to be shed from a holy

Person, and there was only one holy Person who had no sin. He took your sin and mine upon himself by hanging on a cross. Why? Because Jesus couldn't die. Death only came because of sin, but Jesus had no sin, so they couldn't kill Him. He laid down His life by taking our sins upon Him. On that Good Friday, He died so we can live. He went into the grave; the Bible says He descended and got the keys of death and then His resurrection came.

The cross, the Resurrection, were only a means to God's end. It was part of the process to the Kingdom of Heaven returning.

This is the greatest news ever because this is the very act that the Kingdom returned. The cross, the Resurrection, were only a means to God's end. It was part of the process to the Kingdom of Heaven returning. Jesus Christ did all of that so that He could do this one thing in John's Gospel. When Jesus told His disciples to meet Him in Galilee after the Resurrection, all of them were afraid, hiding behind closed doors. The Bible says Jesus walked through the door and said, "Peace be unto you" (John 20:21). They were still afraid. He said it again. When they recognized it was Jesus, He said "Peace be unto you." He asked something to eat and they gave Him something — which is to say that Jesus was in a real body.

In Luke 4:43, Jesus explained that he must preach the Gospel of the Kingdom in other towns because that is the purpose for which He was sent. He accomplished what He said He would with Resurrection completing the task of conquering sin so that the lost may be redeemed. All of was humankind lost when sin was committed in the garden of

Eden. Jesus came and died that we could have life again. Now the Father can live in us; that's why Jesus came. And that's why you have the authority, because the power of the Holy Spirit now resides in us. Jesus said where two or three are gathered in His name, touching and agreeing, you can ask anything in His name, and it will be done.

Do you understand the power of prayer? Do you realize that you are healed? If you're sick, you don't pray a prayer of healing just because you want to feel good. You always pray for healing because you're going to allow Him to use your body to do His will for His name's sake. Then God hears your prayer. Always pray according to the constitution that governs those in the Kingdom. In Matthew 4, before Jesus began to preach for the Kingdom, the Bible said He was tested. A faith that cannot be tested cannot be trusted. Your faith is only as strong as the trials you have already endured. The devil tested Him, but God Himself went back to His Word. He said "It is written that man shall not live by bread alone, but by every word that proceeds out of the mouth of God (Matthew 4:4).

> *A faith that cannot be tested cannot be trusted.*

If you want things to happen, pray the Scriptures because you must give the Holy Spirit something to work with. That's why the Bible says He will bring to your remembrance the things you need in that hour (John 14:26). When you put something in, you can draw something out—study the constitution that governs the Kingdom.

The greatest message ever preached was the Kingdom of heaven has returned. When you understand this, you will not concentrate on hurts, disappointments, and illnesses, but instead you will open the Constitution and let God's Word speak to increase your faith so that you will be able to deal with whatever you must go through. You can cry out to God based on what God said in His word.

All of this is dependent upon a relationship with Jesus Christ. There is only one way into the Kingdom, and it is through Him. Jesus is the door. Jesus is the gate. Jesus is the way. Jesus is the truth. Jesus is the life.

The Just Shall Live by Faith

Now faith is the substance of things hoped for, the evidence of things not seen. For by it the elders obtained a good testimony.
~ Hebrews 1:11

¹Therefore we also, since we are surrounded by so great a cloud of witnesses, let us lay aside every weight, and the sin which so easily ensnares us, and let us run with endurance the race that is set before us, ²looking unto Jesus, the author and finisher of our faith, who for the joy that was set before Him endured the cross, despising the shame, and has sat down at the right hand of the throne of God.
~Hebrews 12:1–2

What do you do when trouble is all around you? What do you do when the circumstances of life are closing in on you and the enemy tries to take control?

Paul challenges the believers in Galatia in the opening verses of Galatians 3, "Who has bewitched you? Did you receive the spirit of God by the Law or did you by the hearing of faith?" The Galatians were troubled, but they needed to be shaken up in their faith. Then, in verse 11 he reminds them that "the just shall live by faith."

The Hebrews had to be challenged in the same way when they were going through difficulties in their lives. Hebrews 10:38 reminds them and us, "Now the just shall live by faith...."

Are you a person of faith? If you consider yourself to be so, why do you entertain the spirit of fear?

Why are we fearful when God's word assures us that no weapon formed against us shall prosper (Isaiah 54:17)? The enemy brought a virus into the 21st century world that caused many people to fear leaving their homes, even to come to the house of the Lord. Some are still not coming to church—because of the spirit of fear.

The Bible said God did not give us the spirit of fear (2 Timothy 1:7), but rather one of power, and of love, and of a sound mind. So, Paul had to pen this letter to two churches. To the church at Galatia, he had to remind them that the just shall live by faith. He had to pen this letter to the church in Jerusalem to the Hebrews to remind them the just shall live by faith.

Without faith, none of us can please God. Without faith, we cannot be saved; the Bible says we are saved by grace through faith and not by our own efforts or works (Ephesians 2:8–9).

So, what is faith? If we're going to live by faith, we need to know what faith is. Hebrews 11 tells us that faith is "the substance of things hoped for, and the evidence of things not yet seen." Let's examine that for a moment.

You cannot have faith if you don't have hope....

You cannot have faith if you don't have hope, which is simply something that you want for the future. I may hope to gain wealth. I may hope to get a job. I may hope to get accepted to a certain college. Those are the kinds of things about which one may have hope for in the future. But faith is taking the future you're hoping for and giving it substance right now. Faith is the right now assurance of one day having what you hope for. Faith is making substance out of hope in order to do what God has called you to do.

So, God reminds us in Hebrews 11:6 that without faith it is impossible to please God. It was by faith that Abel's voice still speaks even after his brother murdered him. It was by faith that Enoch did not see death at a young age—and after living 365 years, God took him without him seeing death. It was by faith that God told Noah that He was going to destroy the world by a flood and Noah began building a ship. The Bible said the ship was 300 cubits, you know how long 300 cubits is? That's 450 feet. I can imagine the people of his day asking, "What are you doing?" At God's direction, Noah built a ship that was a football field and a half long. He built a ship that was 75 feet high toward the sky. It took him years to build by faith what God said in His word.

It was by faith that Abraham left his homeland when God told him to leave to go to a land he had never seen before. God promised to make Abraham's name great. That's why we have the Abrahamic Covenant today.

It was by faith that Moses' parents did not fear Pharaoh and hid him in a basket. It was by faith that Moses crossed the Red Sea doing what God called him to do. It was by faith that the people of God walked around the wall of Jericho seven times, and with a victory shout they praised God and the walls fell. There was not enough time, the Hebrews writer said, to tell of the accomplishments by faith of Gideon, Barak, Samson, Jephthah, David, Samuel, and the prophets.

When Abraham was 100 years old, God blessed him with the child that was promised to him. Abraham was 75 when God had made the promise that he and Sarah would have a baby. For twenty-five years Abraham believed God by faith. Sarah believed God and she was able to conceive by faith. All of this occurred by faith.

It was by faith that Rahab the prostitute hid the spies of Israel and now her name resides in the hall of faith. It will by faith that those who believed what God said did so even though they had their lives taken, sown in half because they believed God. It was by faith. And then in Hebrews 12:1-2, God says, "Therefore, since we are surrounded by such a great cloud of witnesses who live by faith that we are to lay aside every weight and sin that so easily besets us and run with patience the race that is set before us, looking unto Jesus who is the author and perfecter of our faith and who for the joy that was set before him he endured."

Jesus endured the cross by faith so you and I can live by faith. If you're going to live by faith, how do you live? How do you do it? God said we can move mountains if we have the faith of a grain of mustard seed. That's all the faith you need to say to the mountain, in front of you, "Be removed and cast into the sea." Then He says, "If you do not doubt and you say what you believe, it shall be done." You move mountains by your faith.

Five P's of Living by Faith

Let me give you my five p's for living by faith.

A Purpose to Pursue

As a Kingdom citizen, the first thing I want you to know is God has a purpose for you to fulfill. In other words, everyone who claims to know God by faith, God has a special purpose for your life because you are a part of His eternal work as a kingdom citizen. As a Kingdom citizen, we are a colony of heaven because Jesus said "for the kingdom of heaven has returned." The colony of heaven has returned here on earth, so we don't live in the world, we live in the kingdom by faith. That's why He reminds us, "Thy kingdom come. Thy will be done on earth as it is in heaven."

> *The Kingdom of God is God's method or God's way of life on the earth.*

Heaven is a place. The Kingdom of God is God's method or God's way of life on the earth. You see, everything God does is different than the way the world does. And when you've been born again, you no longer live like the world; you live as a part of the kingdom, a citizen living by faith. You ask everything by love through faith because you are a spirit.

First Thessalonians 5:23 says you are a spirit, because before you came to know God, you were dead in your spirit. You understand what I'm saying? You live from the outside in. You live from the flesh. Your soul is your intellect, your mind, and your emotions. So, you live from the outside in—your five senses determine what and how you live, what you touch, what you taste, what you smell, what you see, what you hear. All of this determined your lifestyle in the kingdom of darkness because your spirit was dead. But when Jesus died on that cross, when Jesus walked down into hell, took the keys, got up from the grave, and now those who repent and believe on Him are part of His kingdom. This means your spirit has been born again, and because of that, old things have passed away and all things have become new. Now, suddenly, the Holy Spirit and your spirit begin to take control of the soul and the body. So, you no longer live according to the world; you now live from within. Why? Because the Bible says, "for the spirit of mind is the candle of the Lord that searches the inner part of the belly." Kingdom living is from the inside out. That's the reason why everything about rejoicing—faith, love—all of that is from the spirit. That's why we can say, "I will rejoice" (that's spirit) "and be glad" (that's soul).

Your spirit is supposed to now equip your soul to live by faith. But now you understand that you are now part of God's plan of redemption here on the earth. Now you understand that you are surrounded by a great cloud of witnesses, those who gave their life of faith. Now you to lay aside all the things that prevent you from doing what Christ is calling you to do, because you are at war with your body and your soul.

People give the devil too much credit. He's already defeated.

So why are people at war with him when he's already defeated? The only thing you have to say is "Get behind me, Satan, in the name of Jesus," and he must flee. You must learn how to use the authority that God has given to you in His name. He has given you the power of eternity to use His name to cast out demons. He has given you this authority for a purpose.

We are asking Jesus to do things, but Jesus said, "I have given you the authority. Why are you asking me? I have given you everything you need to redeem this world." But do we believe that? Jesus not only paid our sin debt, but He also bore our sickness and our diseases. If you understand what that means you will not allow the enemy of sickness to always be upon you. Because faith is the substance of things hoped for and the evidence of things not seen.

It is time that you get your spirit to convince the mind and the body of what the Spirit of God has said.

God is saying by His stripes you are already healed. So, do you believe that the problem is your spirit? It is time that you get your spirit to convince the mind and the body of what the Spirit of God has said. Your healing is already there. I have been saying I'm waiting for my manifestation of my healing from my eyes because I'm healed. I'm healed because the Bible says I'm healed.

You see, a lot of people believe in God, but they don't believe God.

Do you believe in God, or do you believe God? You see, a lot of people believe in God, but they don't believe God. What God has said in this word, do you believe Him? Let not your heart be troubled. Do you believe in God? Do you cast all your cares upon Him because He cares for you? Do you believe that all your needs have already been provided? Do you believe that if you seek first the Kingdom of God and His righteousness that all the things you are taking thought of will be added? When does your confession of faith become personal? When do you move toward what He said and confess Jesus? A part of the keys of the kingdom is confessing Him.

God is saying that since we are surrounded by such a great cloud of witnesses, let us lay aside every weight and sin that entangles us, that entraps us. I don't need to go over the weights. I don't even need to address sin; that's the Holy Spirit's job to convict you. It is not my job to judge anyone. That's the problem with us. We judge one another. The only person you're supposed to judge is yourself and you are to pray for one another. God has a purpose for your life. Everybody has a purpose in the Kingdom of God, and it's not to do what I'm doing. It is to do your part according to what He has called you to.

A Person to Prepare

The second P is you as a person must prepare; you must lay aside every weight and sin. You must be equipped to do the work of God. You have to know what is in God's word. The trickery of the devil is he got us to stop bringing our Bibles to church. He's told us "You have the Bible on your iPad or computer. You got the Bible on your phone. Let me ask you a question. Do you read your electronic Bible daily? but you never read it."

God has more than seven thousand promises to us in it. Yet we don't read it. How in the world are you going to live by

All healing is supernatural.

faith if you don't know what He said about your situation? In this promise book, there are over 150 promises on different subjects that God has given to each one of you—about healing. All healing is supernatural. Should we pray for someone who uses medical technology for healing? Yes! Should we pray for the miracle of healing? Yes! The difference in the two is timing. You may be sick, and God will speed up your healing using the medical profession.

But there may come a time when the medical profession will say they don't have anything else to help you and divine healing is the only answer.

When we talk about miracles the only difference is time.

When we talk about miracles the only difference is time. Miracles are happening right now. I may take a week. It may take a year. Or like Abraham, it might take twenty-five years. But the important thing is, do you believe? Do you live by faith?

Understand God has a purpose for you to pursue. You have a person that you must prepare. That means participating in Bible study. It means going to prayer meeting. It means corporate anointing. You can't get everything you need standing at home. You need to come and assimilate yourself with the righteous so that you can get a corporate anointing.

The Bible says (Philippians 4:13), "I can do all things through Christ...." Let me rephrase that verse with another interpretation: "I can do all things through the anointing which strengthens me." Christ is not Jesus' last name; it is the anointing. "I can do all things through the anointing of Christ from Jesus who strengthens me."

A Price to Pay

So, you have a person to prepare thoroughly, and you have a price to pay. Hebrews says, "Let us run with endurance," or "let us run with patience." You will have times in life when you're dealing with difficulties or pain. Yes, you have a price to pay. What's your price? Pain! The devil's greatest motivator to get you to disobey is pain, but for God, pain is the price you pay for faith. You're not the only one who's had pain in your life, but are you going to allow pain to put you on the sidelines? Will you allow pain to stop you from obeying God? Are you going to allow pain to stop you from living by faith?

Don't you think Abraham had pain? Don't you think David had pain? Don't you think Samuel had pain? Don't you think the prophets had pain? Then why do you think you shouldn't have to deal with pain? Let us run this race with patience.

How do you deal with your pain? You look unto Jesus because He gave you power to receive. Look to Jesus. (Notice I did not say look at Jesus.) When Peter looked to Jesus, he was able to step out of the boat and onto the water by faith. But when he took his eyes off Jesus, he began to sink. When you look at your pain more than you look at Jesus, you're going to sink because the problems of the pain will overtake your faith. God is saying, "I have given you faith."

The only way you can have faith is to stop living off yesterday's experience. The Bible doesn't say faith comes by what you have heard. It says faith comes by hearing. It's faith in the present tense. So just because you lived victoriously by faith yesterday, you still have to get up-to- date and live by faith today. You can't live on yesterday's experience. You need fresh mercy. You need fresh manna today. If you don't, the devil is going to whoop your head. You're going to allow him to take control, versus saying "Get thee behind me, Satan."

That's why the Bible tells us that life and death are in the power of the tongue. Many of us are giving too much credit to the devil. Let me give you some examples.

Person 1: "How you feel today?"

Person 2: "I'm sick."

And that's when the devil says, "Do you hear what she said?"

Faith says, "I'm getting better every minute of the hour."

Faith doesn't deny the reality of what you see or are experiencing. But that is only a temporal, transitional reality.

Faith doesn't deny the reality of what you see or are experiencing. But that is only a temporal, transitional reality. You don't give deference to that. You give an attribute to faith, what God said in His word. Find a Scripture passage about what God said and hold on to His Word.

Let me give you some other examples. If you look at your kids and say, "Those are some bad children," you just gave the enemy access to your children.

Or, you tell your wife, "You make me sick." I want you to listen to what you're giving power to by your words. You are a spirit. What comes out of your mouth will manifest what you say. John 1:1 says, that in the beginning was the Word, the Word was with God and the Word was God and the Word became flesh.

If you have a critical spirit, you're going to have a life of being critical, a life of pain, a life of disappointment. Quit saying, I'm just playing the devil's advocate." He doesn't need your avocation. The Bible says let no corrupt communication come out of your mouth (Ephesians 4:29). Do you use sarcasm? Do you try to use a joking manner to tell an untruth? Don't even do that. Spirit people are called to lay aside every weight and sin that easily besets us looking unto Jesus who, with the author and finisher of our faith. Author means He gave you the faith. He is the one who makes your faith complete, perfect.

Romans 12:1-2 says I beseech you brethren and by the mercy of God that you present your bodies as living sacrifices, holy and acceptable to God, which is your reasonable service. Do not become formed to this world but be ye transformed by the renewing of your mind."

God is trying to get you to go back to the mind he gave you in Genesis 1 and 2.

God is trying to get you to go back to the mind he gave you in Genesis 1 and 2. Then He tells you to not think of yourself more highly than you ought (Romans 12:3). Why? Because He gave you the measure of faith. Everything you have come from God. He gave you the faith to be saved. He gives you the faith to be healed. He gives you the faith to lay hands on the sick and they shall recover. He gives you the faith to cast out demons. Do you believe it? It's in His Bible.

Because the question is, do you believe in God, or do you believe God? Looking unto Jesus, who is the author and the perfecter of our faith.

Just remember, you have a purpose to pursue, you have a person to prepare, you have a price to pay and you have power to procure.

Power to Procure

The only way you can receive His Kingdom blessings is to procure them through faith.

God has given you what you need to favorably negotiate all your circumstances. But it's all by faith. The only way you can receive His Kingdom blessings is to procure them through faith. You must know what He said in His Word, promises or covenant. This is no different to citizenship entitlements of a country, such as the United States of America. If you are eligible for Social Security benefits in America, they do not automatically start sending you checks. You have to make a claim. So, it is with faith.

He said His yoke has destroyed the yoke of bondage. And whatever has happened in the past in your life, God will forgive you. The only thing you must do is repent and give it to God and you will be cleansed. But after that, you must learn how to forgive yourself. Paul tells us (Philippians 3:12–14) "forgetting those things which lie behind...." Everything you have done in the past, God no longer remembers it, but the devil always wants to bring it to your attention.

And every time he does, you simply tell him "No weapon formed against me shall prosper" (Isaiah 54:17).

"I have on the whole armor of God (Ephesians 6), Devil, you've got to leave."

"Get thee behind me (Matthew 16:23) in the name of Jesus" and he has to flee (James 4:7) because God said in Galatians 3:13 that Jesus has redeemed us from the curse of the Law.

Read Deuteronomy 28 and all the blessings He told then are still those blessings for you. Then He said if you don't do it, all the curses will occur. The Bible says Christ redeemed us from all those curses—such as sickness and disease. God is saying "I have redeemed you."

Will you live in the kingdom? Will you utilize the keys God has given to you in the kingdom? God has given you the keys of faith by love, and everything that we do must be done in love. We must love one another and quit allowing the enemy to turn us against one another. We must stop using the words of the enemy toward one another. We instead need to say "I'll pray for him. I will pray for her."

When gossip comes up, do not be involved. Do not accuse your brother because you know who the accuser of the brethren is (see Rev. 12:10). So, you have a purpose to pursue, you have a person to prepare, you have a price to pay, you have power to procure and finally, you have a prize to possess.

A Prize to Possess

One day you have a prize to possess, and the reason why you have a prize to possess is because the Bible says that Jesus, who for the joy that was set before Him (Hebrews

12:2), endured the cross. Jesus on that cross took away all our iniquities. He took all our diseases upon Himself. He bore our sin. He died, and three days later, he got up out of the grave on the first day of the week.

He came for this purpose. He found His disciples full of fear, shackled in a room, and He walked through the door. The first thing He said was "Peace I say unto you." Then the Bible said He did something that could not be done since Genesis 1–2. He went to them and breathed the Holy Spirit upon them.

When you are born again, you have the Holy Spirit. That voice is speaking to your spirit, and you must tell the mind and the body to get in order.

Example of a Loving Father

*It was meet that we should make merry, and be glad:
for this thy brother was dead, and is alive again;
and was lost, and is found.*

~Luke 15:32

In Exodus 20, there's a verse of Scripture that says "Honor thy father and thy mother that your days will be lived long here on earth." Of course, when I read this verse, I think about my own parents. Of all the people I've met over my lifetime, my dad is still my mentor. For sixteen years my dad worked two eight-hour shift jobs to provide for his family. My father would come home, having worked the graveyard shift from 11:00 p.m.–7:00 a.m. He would come into our bedroom and say, "Gary, get up! Kenneth, get up!" because it was time to go to Sunday school.

My dad was a great father. He is a good example of what it means to be a father. He not only took us to Sunday school after having worked two eight-hour shift jobs, but he would spend time with us and teach us the Bible. I can remember during those times that he had a book that had a lot of pictures in it and it told the stories about some of the key players in the Bible. We learned about Daniel in the lions' den. We learned about Moses. We learned about Shadrach, Meshach, and Abednego. We learned many things at home, and the reason why that was important was because it's the father's responsibility to teach his children the Word of God.

> *In Jewish culture, it was the responsibility of the father to teach the Scriptures and to train his children in the faith.*

In Jewish culture, it was the responsibility of the father to teach the Scriptures and to train his children in the faith. And at the age of 12 or 13, a bar mitzvah took place where they celebrated the child, coming into religious adulthood because his father had taught him the Word of God.

It's so important for each of us to understand that we must honor our father and our mother every day, not just on Father's Day or Mother's Day, because every day is a day of celebration and a day to honor our parents. In Luke 15, Jesus tells a story about a man who had two sons, and in the story, He shows us an example of a father's love. The youngest son came to his father and said, "Give me my portion of the estate now."

In making this request, he was not honoring his father. He, in essence, was saying, "I no longer want to be a part of this family. I wish you were dead so I can get what will be rightfully mine." The father granted his request, and the Bible says the son left his father's household and went into a far country. He wanted to be on his own and see what the world had to offer. He wanted to experience what his father had probably protected him from. He left his father's love and he recklessly spent all of the resources that had come from his father.

When we read the word "father" in the New Testament, it means "source." Father is the foundation, as Jesus tells us in the Model Prayer, "Our Father…." He is the Source of our strength. He is the Source of our wealth. He's the Source of our comfort. Father is the foundation. But this son in Luke 15 went off and spent all the resources that his father had labored for to develop a legacy for the family.

The Bible said a severe famine over the land came after all his money was spent and no one would give this young man anything to eat or a job. He found himself in crisis. So what did he do? He had left his home training and went to a far country, but because of the father's teaching, because of the father's love, because of the training his father had invested in him, the eventually came to himself while sitting in a pigpen—someplace a Jewish man had no business being. He was so hungry, the Bible says, that he wished that he could feed himself from the pods that the pigs were eating. It was at that moment he had an awakening.

Then the Bible says, "but when he came to himself…." In other words, the Holy Spirit began to work in his heart. The Holy Spirit began to remind him of all the things that his father had taught him as a child. He began to reflect upon the love and the care of his father. He asked himself, "How many of my father's higher servants have food to eat and here I am starving unto death?"

At that moment, the young man did what we call repent. The word "repent" means to change your thinking, to change your attitude. He began to reflect upon the love and protective care of his father, the teaching of his father.

A Father's Love Grants Room for Mistakes

The father's love in Luke 15 allowed room for his son to make some mistakes. When the son came to his father and asked for his portion of the estate, his father did not try to be a holy saint. His father did not try to prevent him from leaving or from exercising his free will. Why? Because the father had already done his job and trained his son in the way that God expected him to live, even though he chose to leave his father's care and go into a far country. But because of his training, because of what his father had seeded in him, the young man began to reflect upon his mistake.

You see, there are times in life when pain will cause you to reflect upon your mistakes. There are times in life when you will become willing to change only because the pain can no longer be tolerated. When the young man repented, his attitude toward his father changed. His attitude toward his family also changed, and he said to himself, "I'm going to go home and say to my father, "Father, I'm no longer worthy to be your son. I have sinned against heaven and against you. But please allow me to be like a higher servant as a part of your family."

Because he had repented, the son had gotten his speech together and his words reflected that his attitude was in the right place. And after he had repented and changed his thinking about his father, he took action. He got up and he headed home. The pain of life had broken him of his pride and brought him to the point of realizing that he did not want to live apart from the love and security of his father's household, and he was willing to change.

A lot of us need to change. We need to come to an understanding that the life that we are living is not the life that we want and that our fathers, our parents, have been trying to instruct us in what thus says the Lord. But because of our pride, we want to do our own thing. But only when his pain got so bad that it could not be tolerated, he decided to change.

That's what repentance is. Repentance doesn't mean that you come down the aisle of a church, grab pastor by the hand crying and saying you want to change. Repentance means you have made up in your mind that you don't like your situation and you are willing to change. Repentance means you have changed your thinking.

Repentance means you have changed your thinking.

The Bible says (Proverbs 23:7, KJV), "As a man thinks in his heart, so is he." Everything which we do starts with our thinking. Repentance means we must change our thinking. Our thoughts affect our outlook. If we think negative thoughts, there may be negative behaviors soon to follow. If we think depressive thoughts, we might end up becoming depressed. That's why the Bible reminds us that we must think on what is good, what is right, what is noble (see Philippians 4:4–8). We have to think on good things, and that's why the Bible exhorts us to bring every thought under captivity.

The son had changed his thinking, so he decided to go home. Notice the father did not go looking for the boy, because he had chosen to leave, but I'm feel confident in asserting that this father was praying all the while his son was gone. This father was concerned about his son. The Bible does not tell us how long he had been gone, but he was away long enough to find himself in bad shape—bad enough to send him back home.

The Bible tells us that the father saw his son coming while he was still a long way off, and the father grabbed his robe, and he began to run toward his son. He had compassion on his son when he got close to him. His son had a repentant attitude and began to tell his father, "I'm no longer worthy to be your son…."

Before he could get the rest of his story out, the Bible says his father grabbed him and kissed him. Then his father told a servant to bring the best robe and put it on him. Why? Because he is royalty. He is part of the family. His father then grabbed a ring and put it on his finger to signify that this was his son. The ring was very significant. It had the father's family emblem on it. Having the ring meant that the son was able to go to a merchant and take the signet off the ring and buy whatever he wanted. He could press it down in wax, which verified that he had rightfully purchased an item because he had the proper authority and access.

When you are in the father's love and the father cares, you have access to whatever you need.

When you are in the father's love and the father cares, you have access to whatever you need. This father commanded, "Put a ring on his finger." Then he said, "Put shoes on his feet, for my son is not a slave. He is my son."

God is waiting for many of us to return to Him. He wants to put a robe on us because we are royalty, because we are His—His sons and His daughters. He has given us full access to everything that He has through the person of our Savior, Jesus Christ. We have access to all that God has to offer us and we're certainly not slaves; we are family.

The first point I want us to understand, the son chose to leave but he repented and he came back.

A Father Forgives

The wayward son's father loved him. The father did not ask what all his son had done while he was away; but rather, his father forgave him as our heavenly Father will forgive us. That's what our Father wants us to do. He wants us to forgive one another as he has taught us in the Lord's Prayer (Matthew 6:9-13): "Our Father who art in heaven, holy is your name. Your kingdom come; your will be done on earth as it is in heaven. Give us this day our daily bread and forgive us of our debts as we forgive others." In the same way, God is saying to us that He will forgive us of our debts—He will forgive us of our sins when we return to Him. In that we see an example of a father's love.

But the story does not end there. As a matter of fact, the broader story is about the Father expressing His love for the lost. The story's context begins when the Pharisees and the scribes began to complain that Jesus was eating and associating with sinners. Then Jesus tells the story of the Father's love in a three-part parable. He first tells the story of a man who had one hundred sheep. One of them went missing, so the man left the ninety-nine sheep and went looking for the one lost sheep. When he found that sheep, he returned, and they rejoiced over the lost sheep who had been found.

The second part of this parable is about a woman who had ten coins. She lost one of them, and the Bible says she put a light on as she swept the house until she found that one lost coin. And then she asked others to celebrate with her. Finally, Jesus told the story of this lost, wasteful son. It shows us that God is concerned about those who are lost. He is concerned about those who don't have a personal relationship with Him and He wants everyone to be in a relationship with Him. The second part of this story is really about the elder son. The father did not show the older son favoritism. That's another point that we need to understand.

A Father Celebrates and Secures

The father had to do a balancing act. Balance the celebration of a son who was lost, but is now found, who was blind, with the securing of the eldest son had been in the fields and never left home. Both sons had problems — one outward, the other inward. The story tells us that the eldest son came back to the house, where he heard music and there was dancing going on. He asked one of the servants what was going on. And the servant told him "Your brother has come back home, and your father has killed the fatted calf and celebrating because he came back safe and sound."

Both sons had problems, one outward, the other inward.

I love how the father gave his eldest son clarity when he did not understand the reason for the celebration. Repentance and redemption are key parts of a divine inspired life. The father said to the eldest son, "all that I have is yours."

So, we must celebrate, and that's the message Jesus was trying to share with the Pharisees and the scribes that we would know the joy of the Lord and that God wants everyone to be in relationship with him.

If you are a wayward child, separated from your father because of pain and disappointment, today is a day that you can return, and you can forgive, you can receive forgiveness, and be reconciled to your earthly father, if he is alive. But you also need to understand that your heavenly Father wants each you to come to him now and be in relationship with Him.

If you find yourself in a difficult circumstance and situation, why don't you try Jesus? John the Baptist proclaimed, "Repent, for the Kingdom of Heaven has arrived" (Matthew 3:2; Matthew 4:17; Mark 1:15). In other words, God is saying that the Kingdom is available to you, but in order for you to enter the Kingdom of God, you must be born again. You must humble yourself before God. Change your thinking. Change your mind. Change your attitude—not to get religion, but to be a part of the kingdom. The only way to do this is through the person of Jesus Christ because He is the way, He is the truth, and He is the life. No man comes to the Father except through Jesus.

If you need to know the heavenly Father in an intimate way, I encourage you to confess with your mouth and believe in your heart that King Jesus died, rose again, and is coming back. Embrace that change in your heart and you will be a part of His Kingdom.

An Attitude of Gratitude

And I will give unto thee the keys of the kingdom of heaven: and whatsoever thou shalt bind on earth shall be bound in heaven: and whatsoever thou shalt loose on earth shall be loosed in heaven.

~Matthew 16:19, KJV

One of the keys of the Kingdom is having an attitude of gratitude and learning how to develop an attitude of gratitude in all things and through all things.

Are you thankful? Do you have a good attitude even amid troubling situations, such as the coronavirus pandemic? Are you able to witness to the world about what it means to be in relationship with Jesus?

We must cultivate an attitude of gratitude because trouble will always be upon us.

Many people died during the pandemic. Many more people got sick. People needed surgeries and could not have them because hospitals were full of patients or surgeries had to be postponed because of the pandemic. Despite all of that, God's people were still able to do the work of the Kingdom.

In Matthew 16, beginning at verse 19, the Bible reminds us that God said He has given us the keys of the kingdom and that whatever we bind on earth has already been bound in heaven. Whatever we loose on earth has already been loosed in heaven.

So, if we're going to develop an attitude of gratitude, it means that we first must be thankful. Thankful for what? It started many years ago with a man named Jesus who was on His way to Jerusalem to be crucified, but instead of going eighty miles south toward Jerusalem, He turned and went thirty miles north to the region of Caesarea Philippi. I sometimes wonder why Jesus, who had to walk more than eighty miles down to Jerusalem, would decide to go thirty miles in the other direction first.

Within the district of Caesarea Philippi was a temple. I can imagine Jesus walking around this Hellenistic temple where the Romans practiced their polytheistic religion. They believed in many gods and I can imagine my Savior walking around the temple complex seeing all those names who claimed to be God. Then He turned to His disciples and asked, "Who do men say that I am?" They replied, "Some say that you are Elijah. Some say that you are John the Baptist or Jeremiah or one of the other prophets."

Then Jesus asked, "Who do you say I am?" (Matthew 16:13–16; Mark 8:27–29; Luke 9:18–20). His quickest student among his disciples, Peter, answered, "You are the Christ, the Son of the living God."

Jesus responded, "Blessed are you, Simon Bar Jonah, for flesh and blood did not reveal that to you, but my Father, who is in heaven. And I say that you are Peter. And upon this rock, Petra, I will build my church, and the gates of the grave, the gates of Hades, shall not prevail against it. Instead, I'm going to give you the keys of the kingdom, and whatever you bind on earth, has already been bound in heaven. Whatever you loose on earth it has already been loosed."

So, what are we doing? Why are we not thankful? According to Shepherds Watchmen *(www.shepherdswatchmen.com)*, in 2020, an average of 1700 pastors quit the ministry each month — one thousand and seven hundred pastors per month left their post! Moreover, an average of 1300 ministers were terminated every month. That means three thousand people of God during every month of the year were no longer at their posts. And even beyond that, 4,000 churches that used to minister in communities, that used to tell the Good News about a man named Jesus, closed their doors.

Despite this, do we not have a lot to be thankful for? I think that we, as God's people, need to be thankful because God has given us an assignment. Yes, in the Great Commission (Matthew 28:19-20) He tells us to make disciples of all the nations, and Baptist them in the name of the Father, and of the Son, and of the Holy Spirit, and to teach them to obey everything that Jesus had commanded.

An attitude of thankfulness begins with us being obedient to the Lord.

An attitude of thankfulness begins with us being obedient

to the Lord. In Matthew 6, Jesus asks, "Why call me Lord if you do not do what I say do?"

It's very difficult for anyone to understand anything about the Bible unless they understand the Kingdom. You see, the Bible is our constitution. The Bible is about the Kingdom and a King. It is about a King and His people, royalty. It is about the King's laws, and the Old Testament is about foretelling that the King is coming. John the Baptist went out as the herald who made the announcement to "Repent, for the Kingdom of Heaven has arrived." If we are going to be on mission with God, we must understand the Kingdom.

I believe the reason why many people are not coming into relationship with the Lord Jesus Christ is because we have not invited them into a Kingdom, but rather into a religion. But Jesus never came to establish Christianity. He did not come to start a religion and be in the same class with Islam or Buddhism or Hinduism. He came that we may have the Kingdom of God returned to earth.

> *...the reason why many people are not coming into relationship with the Lord Jesus Christ is because we have not invited them into a Kingdom, but rather, into a religion.*

Think about it. Whatever Jesus brought to earth with Him is something man had lost. For example, man lost Kingdom rulership in the garden in Genesis 3. Jesus' whole intent in coming to earth was to bring back the Kingdom of God. The Bible says in Isaiah 9, "Unto us a child is born and a son is given and the government shall be about His shoulder." It doesn't say that religion shall be upon His shoulder.

When Jesus said, "I will build my church," understand that church is not a religious word. Jesus only used the word church one time in the Bible, yet the Bible mentions the Kingdom 162 times. I believe we have misunderstood the church to be the Kingdom. The church is not the Kingdom. Think about this. If I were to say to you, "Here is my watch," that implies you may have a watch already. So, Jesus tells His disciples, upon the statement Peter made, "I am the King. I am the Messiah. I am the anointed One." Do you not realize that means King? Jesus came as the King of kings. You must understand the Kingdom if you're going to understand what Jesus has called the church to do.

The word church is the Greek word *ekklēsia (ecclesia)*. It means to call out ones. What does that mean? Jesus was born into a government. Rome was in power, and therefore Jesus was a subject of Rome because Palestine was a colony of Rome. Each colony had governors who had all the authority of Caesar in Italy. They had that same authority in Palestine. So, when Jesus went before Pilate during His political trial, He was crucified because He was charged with claiming to be king of the Jews.

Jesus was crucified for treason because He said that He too was a king. And in the same way that Caesar had his church, Jesus said to them, "I'm going to start my administration." Caesar's senate was called church. It meant his cabinet or his administration. Jesus was telling His disciples, "I'm going to start my cabinet and whatever I tell you to do you must carry out the wishes of the king. So why call me Lord if you don't do what I say?

Jesus was crucified for treason because He said that He too was a king.

Because in a kingdom, if you do not do what the Lord, the owner, the master says, you will no longer be around. That's why Jesus said many would be saying to Him on that day, "Lord, Lord," and He's going to respond, "I never knew you."

Obedience

That's because the first key is obedience. You see, obedience is better than worship. That's what God told Saul—obedience is better than sacrifice. Saul did not do what God told Him to do (1 Samuel 1). He kept what God had told him to destroy and claimed he would use it to worship God. The prophet Samuel responded by telling him that God said obedience is better than sacrifice, which means God is trying to create in us an attitude of being faithful through all things. If we're going to be obedient to God, then we must do what He tells us to do.

What did God tell you to do? The reason why believers may not be making a great difference in the world is because of worry. Yet Jesus said, "Do not worry about these things." He said for us to do one thing: "Seek ye first the kingdom of God and His righteousness and all of these things will be added." Why? Because the Father already knows your needs. The Father knows what's going on through every troubling situation. Everything belongs to God, so if you are in need, all God has to do is move a few resources over to your pocket. And God is never short on resources.

The reason why believers may not be making a great difference in the world is because of worry.

So, God is saying "You have one responsibility if you're going to be my Church, if you're going to do what I called you to do, if you're a citizen of the Kingdom of God." He said, "Your one responsibility is that, every day of your life, you will seek the Kingdom of God." When we do this, we have aligned our lives to the Kingdom in righteousness. So, in order for you to cultivate an attitude of gratitude, you've got to obey God and stop worrying.

That's why He tells us in Philippians 4: "Be anxious for nothing." You see, when troubling things happen, we must adopt the attitude of Psalm 103: "Bless the Lord all my soul in all that is within me. Bless your holy name." And that is a form of "love the Lord thy God with all of thy heart and with all of thy mind, with all of my soul, with all of that strength" (Deuteronomy 6:4-7). And then he said, "Bless the Lord, O my soul, and forget not His benefits."

What is God telling us our benefits are?

Forgiveness — He tells us, number one, our benefits are that He will forgive our sin. You see, we are covered—covered with mire, covered with mess—and when we confess the Lord Jesus Christ, He will forgive us and cleanse us from all unrighteousness.

Healing — He said He has healed our diseases. Many are still working in the church today because God is at work in their life. Jesus reminds us that if we know the truth, the truth will set us free. That's why He said we must worship Him in spirit and in truth, regardless of what the enemy may say.

The enemy is a liar who is trying to dampen our attitude; that's why we need an attitude of gratitude. Every morning when we wake up. When we open our eyes, we ought to say,

> *The enemy is a liar who is trying to dampen our attitude; that's why we need an attitude of gratitude.*

"God, thank You for another day, Lord. This is a day I've never seen before." Please be careful about getting up in the morning, turning on the news and starting your day by filling your mind with all the world's mess. When you do that, all of a sudden, you're going to work but you're not thinking about God. You're thinking about what happened in the community or the nation. God said, "You must seek My face. You must seek My kingdom and My righteousness, and I will guide you in the day."

Freedom from Anxiety — So, do not be anxious for anything, but everything by prayer (Philippians 4:6–7). That means we must pray without ceasing. Prayer must become our lifestyle. It's not something we do; prayer is who we are. We should strive to be in relationship with God every day through prayer.

The reason why we may not be getting what we want from the Kingdom is because we do not understand the keys. Jesus did not preach about being born again. He only talked being born again with one old man who had heard Him talking about the Kingdom in the Temple. Nicodemus came to Jesus at night asking about His kingdom. Jesus told Nicodemus, "The only way that you can see the Kingdom is you must be born again" (John 3:1–21).

Many of us have been delivered, but we haven't been set free. Let me explain what I mean by that. God is in the deliverance. He will set you free and you will be saved. God saved the children of Israel. He brought them out of Egypt, but they still weren't set free because their minds

Many of us have been delivered, but we haven't been set free.

were still on Egypt. God had to take them around in circles until the old minds and mindsets had passed on.

Because of the sin centered around the worship of the golden calf, God allowed that generation to perish, but their seed received the blessing of going into the promised land. They were only forty days away the Promised Land when they walked out of Egypt, yet it took them forty years to get there.

You see, a lot of us have been set free. A lot of us have been delivered. We have been justified before the Father because we have embraced the Lord Jesus Christ as our Savior. But we need to understand that He has some work to do in our lives called sanctification. What do I mean? You're saved, yes, but there are some things in your life He has to wash out from the old life of the world in order for you to become that new creation (2 Corinthians 5:17).

So, when you get saved, you are anxious to get to heaven. But God ain't ready for you to come to heaven. If He was ready for you to come to heaven, He'd just kill you right now. But what God wants you and me to do His work on earth. That's why He gives healing to the body so that you can stay in your body as long as you can so that you can do His will on earth, because you are part of the kingdom.

Do not be anxious for anything, but by prayer and supplication, thanksgiving, in other words, supplication means petition. Realize that the Bible is not a religious book. The Bible is your constitution because you're a part of a government. Jesus, the King, is our elder Brother. Jesus is the Son of God. He is God. He died for us. Since He is the king and we are part of His family, we are members of the royal family. We are a royal priesthood, which means we are citizens of the Kingdom.

You cannot be in the military and be a citizen at the same time. When you are a citizen, it means that you're not in the army. A lot of our theology is wrong. We're singing about being soldiers on the battlefield for the Lord, that we are soldiers in the army of God. That's not biblical. Either you are a citizen, or you are a soldier. Meanwhile the angels are asking, "Why are you trying to do my job?" The Bible said we have the angels as ministering spirits beating on your path.

> *You cannot be in the military and be a citizen at the same time.*

Hebrews 1 says, "Those of us who worship Him must worship Him in spirit and in truth." Why? Because you are Spirit. You are just housed in a flesh suit. There is only one man, that's a species. God made humankind in two forms, male and female. So, in other words, God is trying to tell us the reason why the world is not coming to know Jesus is because we are worshiping unto ourselves as though the Church is the Kingdom.

So, you must be thankful and obey what God has said in His Word. We need to understand that we must learn how to pray and stop worrying. Be anxious for nothing, but by prayer and petition. Petition means legal. That's why He has written a new Covenant with our hearts, a new contract. It means that if you want anything from God, He said ask.

But you have to know what to ask. You have to know what your rights are as a citizen of the United States. Do you

An Attitude of Gratitude

not know your rights as a citizen of the Kingdom? We have a lot of benefits as citizens of the Kingdom that we don't know about because we don't know our rights. The reason why we don't know our rights is because we're not reading the Kingdom's constitution, the Bible. When you understand the constitution, you understand that means petition, which is a legal word. It means that you petition the King, the Judge, for what you want, and with everything you give thanks.

Develop an attitude of giving thanks for everything in advance. Gratitude is the highest form of faith. Start thanking God in advance, before He gives you want and what you need, remembering that a faith that cannot be tested is a faith that cannot be trusted.

Your faith is only as strong as the test you have survived. We have developed this cheap theology, this cheap Gospel, this cheap grace. There are laws in the Kingdom, and Jesus said, "I did not come to destroy the Law, but to fulfill the Law."

In other words, God expects us to do everything He tells us to do. He expects us to love our neighbor. It means that a brother may have a need and you have the resources to meet that need, and you had better keep listening to the Spirit because God may say, "Take that hundred-dollar bill out of your pocketbook and give it to him, because he is part of the Kingdom, as you are part of the Kingdom."

Your faith is only as strong as the test you have survived.

Everything you have already belongs to Him. Jesus told a rich man, "Sell all you have and come follow Me." The Bible says the man got sad because he had a lot of money. That's when Jesus said, "It's very difficult for a rich man to enter the Kingdom of Heaven. It did not say it couldn't be done, but the rich man was unwilling to lay down everything he had to follow God.

Do you realize everything you have belongs to God? So, the next thing you need to develop is the right attitude. Matthew 5 tells us how to develop particular attitudes. Attitudes like, "Blessed are the poor in spirit…the Kingdom of Heaven is theirs. Blessed are those of you who are concerned about others so that you mourn." Jesus said, "You shall be comforted." Then "Blessed are the meek." Meek means self-discipline, self-control, knowing how to manage the resources He gives you. He said, "for you shall inherit real estate." Yes, that's what He said, "You should inherit the earth."

We must understand the necessity of saying "Thank You" to God in all and through all. Your mama taught you to say 'please' and 'thank you.' When you begin to be thankful for the pinto beans and the cornbread on the table, when you learn to be thankful for the car He has given to you, when you learn to be thankful for your spouse… in other words, when you learn to be thankful, then your attitude will change. God is saying when your attitude changes, it means you are now listening to Him. When your attitude changes to, "God, whatever you say is fine with me," then you will be a witness.

The Bible tells us that "after the Holy Spirit comes upon you," if you've been born again, the Holy Spirit will be upon you, "and you will be My witness" (Acts 1:8). He didn't say you're going to go out and witness. He said that because of you, who you are, you are My evidence, you are My witness. Whoever you are standing before, when they see you they

> *Your witness is not just what you say with your mouth, but also what you demonstrate with your life.*

see God. The Spirit of God can emanate from your life to a person who is hurting, to a person who has no hope, to a person who may be ready to give up on life, and God uses you to begin to draw them to Himself. Your witness is not just what you say with your mouth, but also what you demonstrate with your life.

Learn to be grateful. Learn to be thankful, and when you do that, every time you say thank you to your pastor, your spouse, or your children, you are expressing a divine attitude. When that attitude grows, and you realize "Whatever I go through, I can handle it," you are operating with a Kingdom attitude. Thank you, God, because, yes, You healed my diseases. You redeemed me from the pit. You crown my head with love, and You continue to give me all the good things."

> *Everything you need is in the Kingdom.*

Everything you need is in the Kingdom. All your needs are met in the Kingdom. We need to pray regularly, "Thank You for Your Kingdom, Father. Thank You for the key of gratitude. Help me to be grateful because You have given us everything. Help me, Lord, to be thankful. Help me, Lord, to obey You as my King, for You said if we would confess with our mouths and believe in our hearts that Jesus is Lord, we shall be saved."

Jesus died on a cross and took away the sin of the world. Then He got out of the grave and has given the Church authority and power. He has given us His Kingdom.

Living Abundantly

The thief cometh not, but for to steal, and to kill, and to destroy: I am come that they might have life, and that they might have it more abundantly.

~John 10:10, KJV

If you live by faith, you can live an abundant life.

In John 10:10, Jesus said that the devil comes to steal and to destroy. But Jesus came that we may have life abundantly, and more abundantly. If we are going to live an abundant life, we need to confess that there are times in which we worry.

In Matthew 6, Jesus said "Stop worrying." He exhorts us to not worry about what we're going to eat. Do not worry about we're going to wear. Do not worry about these things. And the antidote to worry is to seek first the Kingdom of God and His righteousness and all the things we worry about will be added unto us. So, since Jesus has already given us the antidote, why are we worrying?

In 1988, I had just entered a doctoral program and there was a lot of pressure on me. I was going to be getting married that July, and I began to worry about some things. Then a song came on the radio. It was not a spiritual song, and it didn't say much. The song was by a guy named Bobby McFerrin. The primary message of the song was simple, "Don't worry. Be happy." He didn't tell you what you needed to do to not worry, he just kept singing, "Don't worry. Be happy."

...maturity is the product of good times and challenging times.

You see, maturity is the product of good times and challenging times. As we grow older, we come to recognize that there are times when trouble seems to be hitting us on every side. But in those times, God says to us, "Don't worry. Do not be anxious. Because trouble is inevitable."

Trouble is unpredictable, but one thing is certain—all of us will have trouble sooner or later. All of us go through difficulties in our lives. We never know when we will find ourselves in a troublesome time, but we can be 100 percent certain that it will come. We can be having a good day and, suddenly, one phone call can cause us to find our life full of trouble.

Trouble is unpredictable, and trouble is impartial. Trouble doesn't care that you are handsome, like me. It doesn't care if you are skinny. It doesn't care that you are white. It doesn't care if you are black. It doesn't care if you are Native American, or Hispanic, or Asian. It doesn't care about your career or how much money you make. Trouble simply does not care.

But we endeavor to understand the nature of trouble, we also need to understand that trouble is necessary. If we didn't have trouble, we would not know that God is able—able to give us strength during our traumatic times.

The Bible says when you are weak, tell yourself that you are strong. That's faith! Faith is standing on God's word when nothing around you is pointing toward a hopeful resolution to your problem. That's why God says in Matthew 6, "Don't worry." Don't worry about what you're going to eat. Don't worry about what you're going to drink. Don't worry about where you're going to stay. There's enough trouble in today that you don't need to worry about tomorrow." And then He closes that chapter with, "Seek first the Kingdom of God." When you seek the Kingdom of God before all else, you will learn that everything is going be alright, no matter how things may look in the moment.

Jesus came into the world through forty-two generations, and in Galatians 4:4–7, the Bible says that in the fullness of time, Jesus came. And when He came, He came with a message—the greatest message ever preached: "Repent, for the Kingdom of heaven is near."

Suddenly, after thousands of years, Jesus came and brought the Kingdom of God back to earth. He said in Luke 4:43, "I must preach the Kingdom of God and other towns because this is why I came." In other words, the Kingdom of God means that the people of God have to be careful that we don't do religion.

Religion is saying, "I'm a Baptist," or "I'm a Presbyterian, or "I'm a Pentecostal," or "I'm this or that." Jesus did not come to earth to bring a religion known as Christianity. He came to bring the anointing, to bring the Kingdom of God back to earth that humanity lost in Genesis 3. Because earth is a colony of heaven, the Kingdom of Heaven is a place. Any place in the Bible where you see the Kingdom of Heaven referenced, it means a place. Any time you see the Kingdom of God, it means God's system on earth. It is God's way of doing things, and His way is different than this world's way of doing things.

Jesus taught in Luke 8, that the Kingdom of God is like this: "A man goes out and sow a seed...." Then, in Luke 18:1-8, He taught that the Kingdom of God is like this: "There was the unjust judge, and this woman comes to him...."

The Kingdom of God works differently than the dealings of earth. You are a part of the Kingdom of God. And when you understand that you are part of God's Kingdom, you come to understand that everything you need is in the Kingdom.

Faith is now. Hope is in the future.

The Kingdom is spiritual. It is unseen. And faith is unseen. Faith is now. Hope is in the future. And so, everything God said in His Word, can be believed and accepted as fact. We can stand on the Word of God, but we must live by faith if we're going to have an abundant life.

You Must Be Born Again

The first thing you must do in seeking the Kingdom of God is you must be born again. You must admit that you are ready to repent. What's repent? Repentance doesn't mean to come down the aisle of the church, grab one of the deacons, or grab the pastor by the hand and start crying. Such displays may be a sign of conviction, but it doesn't mean that you have repented. A lot of folks stay caught up in sin deliberately. They get up day after day and say, "Lord, forgive me," and they keep on in their sin because they haven't repented. People must quit playing with God, because God is a king, and everyone is subject to His sovereign authority. In other words, you do what the king says. If you don't do what the king says, you may not be around much longer.

> *The Kingdom of God is not a democracy.*

The Kingdom of God is not a democracy. The King is He is Lord. He owns everything including the citizens. And all rights are surrendered to Him. God is King, and the King said we must submit; we must obey. God expects us to obey Him. So, what do we obey? It means we must have knowledge of God to obey Him, and the depth of our knowledge is dependent upon the intensity of our desire: "Blessed are those who hunger and thirst for righteousness, for they shall be satisfied" (Matthew 5:6).

Knowledge is the light of God and knowledge of God brings understanding. Why? Because you and I are a spirit. Joseph and Mary had to teach Jesus how to be human; in a similar way, the Spirit of God is trying to teach us how to be spirit. God is saying, "You must continue to seek the Kingdom of God and His righteousness."

Righteousness means being put in right position, in right relationship with God, in right fellowship with God. Therefore, your prayer time needs to move from prayer to fellowship, so that you get up in the morning and say, "Good morning, Jesus."

He says to me, "Good morning, Kenneth."

"Lord, what are we going to do today?"

"Kenneth, you tell me what we're going to do today."

Why does He speak to me this way? Because I am a part of the body of Christ, and Christ cannot do anything without His body. He is the Head, but we are the body. The body cannot do anything without the Head, and the Head cannot do anything without the body. And He has given authority to the body here on earth.

The book of Ephesians is essential teaching for every Christian because it is all about the authority of the believer. Jesus gave His disciples a command that we know today as the Great Commission (Matthew 28:19-20). He prefaced it by saying, "All authority is given to me in heaven and in earth" and concluded with, "Now, you go."

We all are waiting on God to do something on earth, and God is waiting on each of us to do something on earth. When we seek first the Kingdom of God then we are in unified relationship with God. We are born again.

Meditate and Study His Precepts and His Promises

You can't study God's Word if you don't read His Word. The problem I see in our country is that we talk about having a relationship with Jesus, but we know very little about true fellowship with Jesus because we don't read His Word. The devil is eating us alive because we don't have

The devil is eating us alive because we don't have sufficient knowledge of who God is....

sufficient knowledge of who God is, and yet everything we need is in the Word.

Utilize the Word

You must take control of your situation by utilizing words — God's Word.

Thinking dominates. This is why we must have the mind of Christ. You must take control of your situation by utilizing words — God's Word. Why? Because He has given you authority and He has given you the opportunity to use His name to do the work of the Kingdom. In other words, you have power of attorney. You can use His name.

But whatever the circumstance, you always need to know what He said in His Word. He tells us how to come that we might have life and more abundantly (John 10:10).

He tells us, "Come unto me, all of you who are weary and heavy laden" (Matthew 11:28-30). He tells us to take His yoke. Why? Because His yoke is easy, and His burden is light. We don't have to heavy bear the weight that comes from the yoke of man.

In Jesus' day, a person would put a yoke around the animal's neck, and it might be unable to bear the weight. But Jesus said, "My yoke is easy." His yoke is easy, but religion makes His yoke hard. Religion gives us all the do's and the don't's. Religion teaches, "You've got to do this. You have to do that." We keep telling people this and then we wonder why folks are not coming into relationship with God. It's because we have all these religious things to do. And they respond, "If that's what it means to be a Christian, I don't want to be a Christian."

God has said we must understand and meditate upon His precepts and His promises. What promise did you call upon today? What have you asked God to do for you today? Every day, God is saying to us. "I have given you power."

Someone reading this may be worried about their children. Some may be worried about the trouble they are going through at work or the situation they are in at church or in the community. But God is saying, "Do you not know they are occupying your house? Do you not know I have given you power to cast spirits and addictions away?"

The problem is most of us have not been taught how to deal with trouble. We have not been taught how to deal with all the negative spirits the devil tries to bring upon us and upon our children. The devil may not be up in them, but the devil might be up on them. God is saying, "Go and lay your hands on that child and cast that spirit away" (Mark 16:17–18).

We haven't been taught the power of laying on hands. There comes what we call in the Kingdom "the period of contact." The anointing of God in your life flows through contact. That's why He said, "Where two or three are gathered…" (Matthew 18:20) in His name, touching and agreeing, He is there also. But you must have faith to do this. I can't have faith for you. You may just be hoping rather than exercising faith, and that means we're not in agreement as believers.

The anointing of God in your life flows through contact.

Let me explain: I can pray, "Lord, I lay my hands on my sister here." I can pray that, according to the Word, that sister is healed." And I could then ask her, "Sister, are you healed?"

"I'm hoping so."

If that is the sister's response, it means we are not in agreement. So how then can healing occur?

That's why Jesus walked in the room of Jairus' daughter and put everybody out—because of doubt (Mark 5:21–43, Matthew 9:18–26, and Luke 8:40–56). We must learn to quit doubting what God says in His Word.

Do you believe in God or do you believe God? Do you believe that what God says in His word is true? If you do, then stand on it! Quit giving too much glory to the devil. I'll give you an example. I can ask someone, "Brother, how are you doing?"

"Aw, Brother, these allergies are just really getting to me."

That brother just gave power to the allergies because he is a spirit. What he said gave empowerment to the allergy.

God works differently in His Kingdom. His Kingdom is not like what we do in the world. You say what you believe, and you mean what you say. That's faith. But you must have knowledge of God's word in order to do that. That's why He said we can lay hands on the sick. He didn't say only the pastor or the preacher or the deacon can lay hands. He said you and me and every other person who believes can lay hands on the sick. All who believe can lay hands on the sick. All who are saved can cast out demons. All who are saved can claim what God says in His Word.

If we're going to live the abundant life that God is calling us to, we must learn how to praise.

Learn How to Praise Him

If we're going to live the abundant life that God is

calling us to, we must learn how to praise. Let me deal with that for a moment. Since you are a spirit, you must make your soul and your body cry out what your spirit is saying on the inside. I don't care whether you are an introvert. I don't care if you are an extrovert. I don't care whether you are an ambivert. I don't care what kind of "vert" you are, you got to praise God for yourself. The praise team can't get up and make you praise God. A lot of your breakthroughs are only going to come when your praise equals your prayer. That's why in the Old Testament they sent out singers in front of the army. Their job was to praise God for the victory before the battle even occurred.

The Bible says the greatest worship leader ever known happened to be a king — King David. Also, the largest book in the Bible is a songbook. David tells us in Psalm 103 that we have to praise God for ourselves. David said, "Bless the Lord, O my soul and all that is within me." David is talking to his soul. He's talking to himself. Likewise, I have to make my soul, my mind, my intellect, and my emotion praise God.

There are more than seventy names for God in the Bible and we must know Him through them.

There are more than seventy names for God in the Bible and we must know Him through them. Let's start calling on Him by all His names. Bless Jehovah Jireh. Bless Jehovah Rapha. Bless Jehovah Nissi. Bless Jehovah Shalom. Bless El Shaddai. Bless Adonai. Bless Elohim. Bless the name of God. Lord, I bless you. Jesus taught us that holy is His name.

Everything within us must bless His holy name, "Bless the Lord, O my soul and forget not His benefits" (Psalm

103:2-5). David reminded himself of God's benefits. When was the last time you remembered the benefits of God in your praise? The first day, he said, "You forgive all of our sins." That's the benefit. Then, "Forgive us our transgressions." He forgives us.

The second thing he says, "No, I can't forget that you heal all our diseases." Now, he didn't say some diseases. He said all. We are compounding diseases upon diseases because we believe the report of someone other than the Lord. I'm not saying I don't believe in medical science. I believe in medical science. But what I'm saying is that we'd rather believe the doctor's report than the Lord's report. The first time you go to the doctor's office, he or she comes in with a pad and asks if anybody in your family has diabetes or if anybody in your family has cancer. You start claiming, "Yeah. Yeah. My mother, my daddy. Yeah, yeah, yeah."

So, whose report will you accept? Do you believe God said that by His stripes you are healed (Isaiah 53:5)? Believe God's report. I am a witness that God does give healing.

The third thing David says is that God redeemed your soul from destruction. You ought to praise Him for redeeming your soul from destruction. God redeemed your soul from hell through the work of Jesus. Redeemed you to purchase you again. He owned us in Genesis 1:2, and man lost it in Genesis 3, so He had to purchase us again. That's what we call redemption. He bought us back. He said, "You are not going to be destroyed, because I redeemed you from destruction."

Fourth, he tells us what not to forget. Don't forget that you need forgiveness. Don't forget that you need healing. Don't forget that He has redeemed your life from destruction.

And then he tells you God has crowned your head with steadfast love. David tells us about God's love—for God so loved the world He gave His only begotten Son to the world (John 3:16). Faith works by love. He tells us that we must love the Lord our God with all our hearts and with all our soul and mind (Deuteronomy 6:4-5; Matthew 22:37) and our neighbor as ourselves.

Do you love your neighbor as yourself? That means if your neighbor has a need, and you love yourself, then you ought to be able to help meet that neighbor's need, just as you would meet the need in your own life. That is one of the keys of the kingdom. The problem is we don't believe. The Bible tells us to owe no man anything but to love. So that means everybody who is part of the Kingdom should get out of debt. I'm going to repeat that. Everybody who is part of the family of God is supposed to be working to get out of debt so that we can be free to do what God has called us to do. For instance, if a pastor tells the congregation, "We owe $300,000 on this church," every person in there should be able to put their money together and pay off the indebtedness. But we have not been taught that.

> *Everybody who is part of the family of God is supposed to be working to get out of debt so that we can be free to do what God has called us to do.*

Romans 13:8 says pay your taxes. Pay your revenues. Give respect and honor to those who need respect and owe no man anything but to love him. That's the Bible. So, we ought to be working to get out of debt. The problem is that we are worried about what other people think about us and not worried about what God has told us to do. If you're going to live the abundant life I'm talking about, you have to live in abundant life by faith.

That means you must first stop worrying. There's enough trouble today that you don't need to worry tomorrow. You're worried about what you're going to eat tomorrow, but you know you got some pork chops at home today. Some of us worry from one meal to the next meal. Some of us are worrying, "What I'm going to eat tomorrow?" when tomorrow is not even promised to you. What I'm going to wear to work tomorrow? Well, wait till tomorrow. You likely already have enough clothes in the closet to go find something to wear and you don't have to say "I don't have anything to wear" when you have a closet full of clothing.

When I got married, there was one thing I learned quickly—that I could not stop my wife from shopping. I said to myself, "I'm not going to try to stop her from shopping. I'm just going to join her." I learned many years ago that I'm not going to allow shopping to mess up my marriage. I'm just going to make some more money. Quit worrying and quit using credit. Pay your credit cards off. Pay your house off. Pay your car off. It may start with paying the coffee table off first, and then maybe you need to move around the room and pay the sofa off next. Maybe you need to move in the kitchen and pay the refrigerator off after that, and so forth.

How can you live an abundant life if you have the pressures of debt upon you? Couples must work together as husband and wife. One cannot be saving while the other going into that same pot taking out.

A lot of the problems we have in life, we have brought it upon ourselves. That includes a lot of the problems with our health. Recently, the Lord began dealing with me about my weight. The Lord said, "You know what you have to do."

I said, "Yes, Sir."

He said, "You've got to get healthy." You know that you have to have divine health in order to have a divine life. You've got to bring your health under control. You know that don't you?"

"Yes, Sir."

"You know your body is the temple?"

"Yes, Sir. Yes, Sir. I know."

"So, what you gonna do about?"

I said, "Lord, I need your help. I need your help."

If you're going to live the abundant life, you have to understand the knowledge that God has given you. Don't substitute what He has said and what He has told you to do in His word and think you can go to Scripture and claim that Scripture when He is saying "You've got to obey the information I've already given you."

> *...if you're going to live the abundant life, you must be born again.*

So, if you're going to live the abundant life, you must be born again. If you're going to live the abundant life, you've got to meditate and study His precepts and His promises. If you're going to live the abundant life, you need to learn how to give Him praise. You have to praise Him for His forgiveness. You've got to praise Him for your healing. You've got to praise Him because He has redeemed your soul from the pit. You've got to thank Him for His continued love and steadfastness. If you keep reading the text, He goes on and tell us that He satisfies our mouth. He tells us when we don't forget His benefits, He will restore our youth like an eagle. He said, "Bless the Lord." In other words, God is saying, "Praise Me when you're going through your troubled times, and I will give you peace. Learn how to use My Word in your difficult situations."

Learn how to use the Word in a challenging marriage. Learn how to use the Word when a rebellious child is not doing what you know that you have trained that child to do. Use the Word when you have conflict on your job. The depth of your knowledge is dependent on the intensity of your desire. Blessed is he that hungers and thirsts for God's righteousness (Matthew 5:6), and He said, "You will be satisfied."

The prosperity that comes from God's Word begins with unconditional obedience.

The prosperity that comes from God's Word begins with unconditional obedience. You will never have enough money if you live off 100 percent of what you have. You never will have enough, because in the system of God's economy, 10 percent starts at the House of God. If you give Him the ten, He will not allow the devourer to eat up your ninety. And then He will open a window and pour out some favor on your life. If you're not a tither, you never will prosper in the way God desires for you to prosper. I didn't say tip God. I didn't say have an attitude of, "I'm not going to give because I don't know what the church is going to do with it." It ain't yours anyway! And if you will learn in God's Word the four types of giving — tithes and offerings, first fruit offerings, alms or giving to charity, and then the Bible talks about seed sowing. Because everything starts with a seed.

You are here today because of a seed, and God is saying, "You must sow into fertile ground and when you sow and give into fertile ground, He promised to give you thirty, sixty, or one hundred times more. So that means if you sowed into fertile ground and you sowed 10 percent, that's a 100 percent return. You have given your ten percent so now you got a hundred and ninety percent.

God's economy is counterintuitive to the world's economy. The world says, "Hold onto what you have," but God says, "Open your hand." So, if you see somebody in need, give. Don't worry about whether they're going to drink it up because you are not responsible for what they do. You are only responsible for what you do.

Remember, if you're going to live an abundant life, you must seek first the Kingdom of God. You must put God first in your life. You must first come to know Him. I once heard a story that the devil tries to convince you that hell is real, and that God is real, but you don't have to be in a hurry to seek His Kingdom.

The more you live for Him, the more God is calling you, "Come unto me, and I will give your life the abundant life that you want."

You don't have to live in bondage. You don't have to live with strongholds on your life. When you give your life to Jesus fully and completely, He will show you what is really means to live, and life abundantly.

Living by Faith in the Kingdom

For she said to herself, "If only I may touch His garment, I shall be made well."

~Matthew 9:21, NKJV

In the Bible, there is a story about an unnamed woman. Scripture does not tell us her name, but history tells us her name is Veronica. This woman was living with a lot of pain. She was sick and had been to every doctor she could. Furthermore, she had spent all her livelihood trying to get well. The Bible says that she had an issue of blood, or a hemorrhage. She had suffered with this condition for twelve years. Image how weak we become when we lose blood. And because of her hemorrhage she was considered unclean.

Imagine not able to go to the house of prayer for twelve years. Imagine the pain and difficulty she experienced in her day-to-day living. But the Bible says she heard about a man. She'd heard that a holy man named Jesus was in town. She heard He was a healer. Suddenly, her hope was renewed. She mustered up enough faith to convince herself, "If only I could touch the hem of his garment, I will be made whole." Her faith gave her the motivation to leave her home in search of Jesus.

Her faith that took her out of her house, knowing that she could be stoned for disobeying the law. But because of her need, because of her belief, and because of her faith, she was willing to take a chance. I can imagine her telling herself, "I will come out of the house, and I will get closer to him. I'll just reach down and touch the hem of his garment and get my healing and go back home. If I do it quietly, no one else will know."

I can imagine that when she got close enough to Jesus, she discretely reached down and touched the hem of his garment. Suddenly she felt virtue and power over all her life, and she knew that she was healed. Meanwhile, Jesus, who had all people around him, pressing against him on every side stopped and asked, "Who touched me? For I felt power leave my body." He began to look around to see who it was in the crowd.

The disciples had no idea what their Teacher was talking about. They may have been thinking, "Surely in the thick of this crowd a lot of people have touched you." Jesus had to help them understand that He was talking about a different kind of touch. He was determined to call out the person who touched Him. Then, the woman stepped out from among the crowd and identified herself as the one who had touched Jesus. She fell at his feet and told Him all about her situation. Then Jesus said to her, "Daughter, your faith has made you whole." With a single act of determination, this woman demonstrated what it means to live by faith in the Kingdom of God.

The first verse of Hebrews 11 tells us that faith is "the substance of things hoped for, and the evidence of things not seen." Faith is the reality of things hoped for, but the confidence of things not seen. Faith is the assurance of things hoped for, but the conviction of things not seen. The Bible tells us that faith is making substance of what you are hoping for and understanding that you have received it before you have evidence of it.

In other words, God is saying that for us to have faith, we must first have hope. Most of us think hope and faith are the same thing. A great reason why we are not accomplishing and receiving what we need, despite thinking we have faith, is because we don't have hope. The word hope indicates future tense. Our hope to get a job. Our hope is to go to college. Our hope is that someone we love is healed. Conversely, faith deals in the now. The problem many of us have is that we are living out the experience of our faith from yesterday, yet we still need faith today. We had faith yesterday, and that's good. But we need new mercies every day. Faith right now is the things you been hoping for and the evidence of things not seen.

Hebrews 11 recalls many of the faithful men and women of the Bible who were able to accomplish great things by faith. One man we learned about is Enoch, who lived by faith. Abel lived by faith to the point that he lost his life. Yet the Bible says he is still speaking even today. Noah lived by faith, having been warned by God of things that were going to occur. He believed and had faith in God and spent years building an ark in preparation of the fulfillment of God's word. I'm sure he must have endured ridicule and scorn from people as they saw Noah going about his work. "What's wrong with that man? Why is he building a boat? We haven't had rain in years, yet he is building a boat." Can you imagine the ridicule he took for acting on his faith?

You probably can imagine the ridicule that Abraham took for his faith when God told him to leave his homeland, not knowing where he was going. He only knew that God had promised to give him a land for him and his descendants.

Can you imagine his wife, Sarah asking him, "Where are we going?"

"I don't know."

All Abraham knew was that God had told him to go, and he obeyed God. Imagine when God came to him at 75 years of age and told him He was going to have a baby. And Sarah, who was age 65 laughed and said, "You've got to be kidding!" But then the Lord spoke to her and suddenly she had faith to believe. Imagine all the men and women during the time of the judges, when everybody was doing what they thought was right in their own eyes. Even they had faith. Moses had faith, to the point that his parents hid him even though they knew they could have been killed for disobeying Pharaoh. They hid Moses because God had a special purpose for his life.

Imagine a prostitute whose name is in the Hall of Faith. Rahab had the faith to believe and hid the spies to keep them from being found. She had faith.

Throughout Hebrews 11, stories are recounted about men and women who lived by faith. Many were standing on the promises of faith to the point that they lost their lives. Others suffered horrific consequences for their faith—

sawed in half, children taken away from them—all while they waited on the promise of God. They lived by faith, and the Bible tells us "Therefore, all of these who are in the clouds are witnesses that you just heard about. Since they lived by faith, you too must live by faith. You must live by faith in the Kingdom of God, because the Kingdom of God is here."

The Kingdom of God is for all of us. The Kingdom of God means that we have lost brothers and sisters who are not part of the Kingdom and by faith we are to go and rescue them because we live by faith.

So, let us review the five points I want to leave with you regarding living by faith in the Kingdom.

God has a purpose for you to pursue.

God has a purpose for every person's life.

Every person who has been born on earth has a purpose. God has a purpose for every person's life. The problem is that often we do not understand His purpose. Often the purpose God put in our lives involves things and dreams that he put in our hearts when we were kids. And sometimes parents can inadvertently we take that purpose out of their children's lives by saying, "You can't make a living doing that." We unknowingly take the dream away from them even though God was calling them for that very purpose.

We have separated our everyday lives in church from our daily lives and work. That was never the intent because God to earth as a man to bring religion. God came to bring His Kingdom back. He came to bring a government back and because of the Kingdom of God, God wants you to understand that if you are working in the health profession, that is your purpose. So by faith, show the love of Christ even in that profession. Go into your world of medicine with faith. Go into your world of education with faith. Go into the world of social work with faith. Whoever you are and wherever God places you, live by faith every day of your life.

We need to live in the awareness that we are a spirit housed in a dirt suit. When we are not born again, when we don't have faith to live for God, we live from the body, soul, and a dead spirit. When a spirit is dead, it doesn't tell you to do anything but bad stuff. Therefore, you did what was right in your eyes. But when you are born again, when your spirit is born again, God says, "Your spirit must sanctify your soul." Now your soul communicates with the body, so you live from the inside out, not from the outside in. First Thessalonians 5:23 tells us that we are spirit, soul, and flesh. Your spirit has been born again and now your spirit communes with the Spirit of God.

Proverbs 20:27 tells us, "for the spirit of man is the candle of the Lord. He searches the inner part of the belly." So, God's Holy Spirit connects with our spirit and our spirit is able to sanctify. That's why the Bible says, "work out your salvation with fear and trembling" (Philippians 2:12). When you've been born again, your spirit must sanctify your mind, sanctify your intellect, sanctify your will, sanctify your emotions. You are no longer living by your emotions; you are now living by the Spirit in the Word of God.

Why? Because God has as purpose for your life. You may think your purpose is insignificant, but no one is insignificant when that person is living in his or her purpose. You may be saying, "God, why did you get me on this job?" God answers, "Because there's a purpose. Because of your life, I may be able to raise new disciples because of your walk with me."

Hebrews 12 opens with, "Wherefore, since we are surrounded by all of these men and women in this cloud of witnesses looking down on us, telling us to run the race that is set before us...." That means my momma is there running her race. My daddy ran his race. My brother is in the cloud of witnesses saying "Get it! Run that race that God has called you to do! Live by faith in the Kingdom of God!"

God has a person for you to prepare.

We must be equipped to carry out the will of the father. We must be very careful because when we live for the world, the world controls our thinking and our emotions. We must be careful what we take into the eye gate, what we take into the ear gate. Why? Because the enemy is the spirit of darkness.

...darkness means ignorance. We are of the Kingdom of Light...

Remember, darkness means ignorance. We are of the Kingdom of Light, which means knowledge, reverence, patience, and understanding. And the devil uses all kinds of tools to keep us in darkness—the tool of social media, the tool of television, the tool of Netflix. We the people of God are now taking in all this stuff that is contrary to the Word of God. It is going into our eye gate and we are feeding the old nature more than we are feeding the soul in the spirit of Christ. Why? Because faith comes by hearing the Word of God. And we wonder why we don't have a victory in our lives. We wonder why our life is not full of abundance. It is because we feed our soul one day a week, and we are feeding the flesh seven days a week.

God is saying you have a person to prepare. How? First, you must lay aside every weight and sin that entraps you, that besets you, that ensnares you, that causes you not to be as effective as you can. So that's why God has said, some of the weights that they're carrying are causing you to not be as effective. There's nothing wrong with a football game. There's nothing wrong with playing soccer. There's nothing wrong with putting your children in baseball. But if those things are causing you to not run your race, and live by your purpose, that can be a weight. Anything that is slowing you down from being all that Christ is calling you to be is a weight.

Many years ago, there was a track athlete named Carl Lewis. He was fast, and he won a lot of gold medals. The television would show Carl Lewis coming into the stadium with his Jheri® curl and his warm-up suit on. He'd be walking around and waving at everybody as he was coming into the stadium to get ready to run his race. Then he would go back into the locker room. Suddenly, he would come out of the tunnel. The warm-up suit was gone. He wasn't waving at anybody anymore. When he came out of the tunnel, he was wearing running clothes made of skin-tight material. He came out with no socks on and no track shoes on. He'd stretch his legs and do everything he needed to get ready. Before he hit the track, he had gotten rid of all the unnecessary weight for him to run his race to win. And that is what God is saying—we must get rid of the unnecessary weight to run our lives in this kingdom.

> *You cannot have faith and worry at the same time.*

Another one of the unnecessary weights we carry is the sin of worry. The reason why many of us are not having the victorious life God has promised is because we worry all the time. You cannot have faith and worry at the same time. God says (see Matthew 6:25-34): "What are you worrying about? You don't have to worry about what you're going to eat. You don't need to worry about what you're going to wear. You don't need to worry about where you're going to stay." He even gives the illustration of how beautiful the lilies are. The only thing He tells us to do is to seek first the Kingdom of God and His righteousness and all our needs will be provided. It is up to us to believe His words or not.

Human beings worry, yet the Bible says do not be anxious for anything (see Philippians 4:4–8). Do not worry about anything. How does the Bible tell you to deal with worry? By prayer, by supplication, by being thankful to God. You can begin by expressing gratitude for the daily blessings you receive: "Thank You, Jesus, for what You have done today. Thank you, Jesus, for waking me up. Thank you, Jesus, for giving me a morsel of bread. Thank you, Jesus, for my family. Thank you, Jesus, for life." When you keep thanking Him, you get caught up in praise and just thanking Jesus.

Now, the Bible says if you have any requests, let them be made known. And the peace that you had from worry will take over. The peace of God shall guard your spirit, heart, mind, and soul in Christ Jesus. Then Scripture you to get your thinking straight. Think on these blessings, these positive things instead of what you're worrying about.

Think on what is good. Think on what is pure. Think about what is holy. That is how you deal with the sin of worry.

If you are still worrying, that means you still have something to work on. You must be able to go to the Word of God and find scripture to address whatever you're dealing with. If you're worrying, go to the Bible to deal with worry, anxiety and God will give you peace. Some are dealing with the sin of unforgiveness and wonder why God is not hearing their prayers. But if you don't learn to forgive, God is not going to forgive you. So, God is saying that the way you forgive others is the same way He is going to forgive you.

Forgiveness is one of the keys of the kingdom. Forgiveness is not for the other person; forgiveness is for you! You had no control over what another person did to you. You had no control when your spouse came in and asked for a divorce. Yet, you're harboring pain, anger, and resentment from thirty years ago and you still can't forgive. Then you wonder why you're not living a victorious life in the Kingdom of God. He is saying you are harboring the weight of unforgiveness. And everywhere you go, that big old boulder you are dragging around with you, is hindering you. That's why you can't run your race. A big ol' 50-pound boulder that you carry everywhere is too heavy for you! Forgiveness is necessary for you to release the weight in the Kingdom of God. Those things are in the past. Do not allow what happened in the past to hold you hostage in the present.

Scripture tells us this way, "forgetting those things which are behind" (see Philippians 3:13–14). How do you deal with that? Bible says you reach forward. You strain forward to the things of God that are ahead. Stretch forward and reach for the glorious days, the victorious life. Reach forward for the faith that you want in Christ—for the things you

> *Live by faith in the Kingdom of God and get rid of the sin of worry.*

are hoping for. Reach forward, and as you reach further, go on to win the prize of the high calling of God. Live by faith in the Kingdom of God and get rid of the sin of worry.

You also must get rid of the sin of unforgiveness, or an offended spirit. The Bible tells the story of a guy in Luke 15, who was comfortably living in his father's household. There were two sons in the father's house. One son goes to his father and says, "Give me my portion of your estate now." He was going to inherit a portion when his father died, but he wanted it right away. His father gave it to him and the son went into a faraway country, living in sin.

Sometimes children may be living in sin, despite having been raised to live righteously. One day, through memory, through training, because of what you put in them, they will make their way back to righteous living. The Holy Spirit can take those memories of Bible truths taught and those experiences of righteous living and make them come to their senses. They will come back to the Father and say, "I'm no longer worthy to be your child. Make me like one of your hired servants." But when you are a child of God, He says, "My child is not a slave. He was lost, but now he is found. Yes, he was blind, but now he can see. Put shoes on his feet so he is not a slave. Put a robe on his back because he is part of the king's family. Give him a ring that signifies he is my son. He can go to any merchant that he wants and buy whatever he wants. He can take that symbol of this family, press it into some wax at a store and buy anything he wanted. Why? Because he was a part of the family.

But there is more to the story of this son who returned to his father's household repentant. It's also about a person with an offended spirit who was unwilling to forgive. When the older brother heard music and dancing going on at the house, he asked a servant, "What's going on?"

The servant told him, "Your brother has returned home, so your father killed a fatted calf to celebrating his return."

The eldest son was upset that they were celebrating because he had an offended spirit. There are four things you can see about an offended spirit. First, the oldest son got angry, and anger is the first sign of hurt, pain, and often of an unwillingness to let it go. Second, the Bible says he refused to go into the house and join the celebration. He isolated himself from his father. Third, while he sat alone sulking, the son was engaging in self-pity. "Oh, poor me. Father, you wouldn't even give me young goat to have a party with my friends, but as soon as this boy returns home, having spent all your money on prostitutes and wild living, you killed a fatted calf. And that's the fourth characteristic of an offended spirit — accusation. The older brother represents religion. Religious people will seek to limit your faith by accusation. The Bible never told us what the boy did in the far country. We only know what his brother accused him of doing. And the oldest son could only speculate about what his younger brother had spent the money on.

Religious people will seek to limit your faith by accusation.

Each of us must lay aside every weight and the sin that entangles us, that traps us, holds us down, and keeps us from living with purpose in the Kingdom of God. God has given you His protection.

You have to quit being so fearful, living as though we do not know you have divine protection. Do you not realize that you are a spirit and that you have some soldiers? The soldiers are sitting around saying, "When is she ever going to ask me to do something for her? God, what's going on with your folks down there? I am ready to work but they don't do anything, even though the Bible tells them there's an angel to help them" (see Hebrews 1). The first chapter of Hebrews tells us that angels are ministering spirits sent to give protection for those who are heirs of salvation. Yet, we don't command them to make use of their authority to help us.

Let me give you an example. You go at work and people are acting hellish in everything, but you don't bind them up. You allow it to go on. That's your fault. That's not God's fault. He has already given you the power of eternity to bind it up. But you must learn a little about faith to believe that. You have to live out that power. Whenever I get on an airplane, I pray, "Ministering Spirit, go before me and keep this plane in the air." When the weather gets choppy and the plan experiences turbulence, I'm not afraid. I know those ministering spirits are doing their job because I have already commanded them in the name of Jesus because He has given me the power of eternity to use His name to do His will. Second Timothy 2:4 reads: "God did not give us a spirit of fear." Paul uses the word spirit. Fear is a spirit, but God has given us power and of love.

God did not give us a spirit of fear and the reason why we become afraid is because of what we take in. If you listen all day to the news, they're talking about negativity. But we take in all this negativity to the point that we begin to pay more attention to that than anything else.

Faith comes by hearing (see Romans 10:17) for the Christian and the Kingdom of God people by the Word of God. Faith comes for the enemy, by hearing what he is telling you. Who are you going to believe? Don't allow the spirit of fear keep you from running the race that God had called you to run.

We have a price to pay.

God has a purpose for us to fulfill; for us to pursue. Number two, God has a person for us to prepare. Laying aside the weights and get rid of the sin. Number three. We have a price that we must pay.

God never told you that when you're living in the Kingdom of God you're not going to have pain. Scripture says it this way. Let us run with endurance. Let us run with patience the race that is set before us. In other words, you got to learn how to deal with your pain. It is not ironic that more older people are in the house of prayer. And you're asking, "Why are older people in the houses of prayer?" It's because they have learned how to deal with their pain. And they give us His spirits to say, "Sir, you don't have to deal with that if you do that. Why don't you do this? Why? Because they have already lived. While we're trying to get where they have already been.

Think about it this way. You enter the race as a young little whipper snapper and you take off running. Then you pass Grandmama and start running backwards, waving at Grandmama as you seem to sprint farther and farther ahead of her. Meanwhile, Grandmama is just making her way, just moving on down toward her finish line. But you're a young whipper snapper and you're running fast. Boy, you're sprinting.

Meanwhile, Grandmama knows it's a marathon and not a sprint. She's just running her with patience while you're sprinting. Then Grandmama comes on down the road and catches up to you. Then she starts trying to walk with you a little bit. But you're not able to say, "Grandmama, I'm beginning to understand what you're talking about now."

We all have to run with patience. We have a price to pay. We have to deal with our pain. We have to deal with struggles. But no matter what, we don't stop running the race!

Grandmama knows when to sit down and take a break, get some rest, and get herself some water. Because she's going to run with endurance, with patience. That's what God is saying to us—run with patience and endurance for the purpose that is set before you.

Number four: Grandmama might have been dealt some terrible blows in life, but she kept running her race. All kinds of things come up against us in life. There are trials everywhere, but Grandmama's not worried about it. She just stays the course. But how was Grandmama able to do that? Grandmama could do that because her eyes were looking at Jesus, who is the author and the perfecter of our faith.

When you're looking at Jesus, by faith you can say, "Storm, get out of the way," because God has given you dominion over the fish of the sea, the birds of the air, every creeping thing, and all the cattle. He did not give you authority over mankind; but rather, He gave you authority over all the elements. By faith, you must pull it down out of heaven to make it happen. You have power to receive because the Kingdom of God is within you. Because God is king, He has a kingdom. Jesus preached the Kingdom of God because He is the king. He has a kingdom, and we are citizens in that kingdom. We are ambassadors.

An ambassador is very important. When an ambassador of the United States goes to another country, he does not go there to speak for himself or herself. That ambassador goes with the full weight of the United States government on his shoulders. So, if someone from that country slapped the ambassador, that person also slapped the United States of America. That one slap will wake the army, the Navy Seals, the and the Air Force. You just woke up the army. You just woke up the Navy Seals. You just woke up the Air Force. The person who slapped the ambassador from the United States, incurred all the weight of the government will come down upon him. When you are an ambassador of Christ, you have angels all around you.

When you are an ambassador of Christ, you have angels all around you.

Elijah's servant grew afraid when he saw the Syrian army on all the hills (see 2 Kings 6). Elisha was not worried. He told the servant, "Do not fear, for those who are with us are more than those who are with them" (v.16) Then he just prayed for the Lord to open his servant's eyes. And when the saw, he said, "Whoa! All the chariots of fire. All the angels are ready to go!" When Jesus was going to trial, he said to Pilate, "Did you not know I can call down some angels?" (Matthew 26:53). Jesus was not here on earth by Himself. The host of angels was here with Him when Jesus was born. Jesus was a rich baby because God took out of somebody else's pocket and brought it to his pocket—gold, frankincense, and myrrh. The Bible says there was a host—an army—of angels talking to the shepherds. The only thing Jesus had to do was issue the command and His soldiers would be taking care of business.

When you look unto Jesus, you have power. When demonic spirits come after you, just start praying to God, "Demons get behind me right now in Jesus' name!" And guess what? They will have to shut up. That's living by faith in the Kingdom of God. Your heavenly Father has given you the authority because you have been born again. He has placed His Spirit in you. His Spirit, the Paraclete, is beside you. The Paraclete is the One who walks beside you. He is one who interprets what is going on. The Paraclete will work as your paraphrase when you have hurt and pain in your life and the only thing you can do is say, "Umph." When you look unto Jesus who has given you power when you are hurting. When you have made mistakes and you need help, the paraclete will be your parachute. A parachute doesn't stop you from falling, but it eases the impact of the fall.

When my wife and I lived in New Orleans while we were teaching at New Orleans Baptist Theological Seminary, it used to get hot. New Orleans had a major bus line that a lot of people relied on for transportation. As you're driving along, you can see people standing at bus stops with something that looks like a yellow or light-colored umbrella. It was a parasol. It keeps people from getting too hot while they wait for their bus to come.

When you're looking unto Jesus, when life gets hot and you don't know how you're going to make it, you need to know what's called the Paraclete. He will work as your parasol and shelter you from the difficult heat of pain. The Paraclete can also work as your paramedic. You or someone you know may be struggling with an illness and the doctors have said there's nothing else they can do. Yet by faith, God said that you are already healed. The Bible said that by His stripes you were healed. The Bible tells us that we can cast all our cares upon Him. Because He cares for us.

The Bible says that Jesus has already redeemed humanity from the curse of the Law. The question is, do you have faith to believe without doubting? For example, your pastor can come and by faith prayer for your healing. Notice, if you are not a person who knows the Lord, or if you are young in the faith, the Lord may heal you based on your pastor's. Then, after you've been walking with God for a while, your pastor may come to you and pray with you, but now you must rely on your faith; the pastor only has to agree with you concerning your healing. You must believe for yourself, and He will agree with two or three gathered in His name, agreeing and touching in the Spirit.

God will do that for you, but you've got to have faith. But if your pastor prayed by faith and you respond, "Pastor, I'm hoping that I'm healed," you didn't get healed. Your pastor was praying because he believed that you would be healed. But if you're still hoping, there's no agreement. You must believe, looking unto Jesus, not looking at Jesus. A lot of folks are just looking at Him. They're not trusting Him.

They're not obeying Him. They're just looking at Him. But God is saying you have power to receive.

If you live by faith in the Kingdom of God, He has a purpose for your life. You must continue to prepare your life because you can't live off yesterday's faith and yesterday's experiences. You need active and living faith. It is ironic to me that when I go to churches now, no one has a Bible,

> *There are 7,000 promises that God has put in [the Bible] to cover every situation that you need.*

yet that is our constitution. There are 7,000 promises that God has put in there to cover every situation that you need. You must go to Scripture and find a passage according to your circumstance and read that Scripture. Put into your eye gate; put it into your hearing. Faith comes by hearing the word of God, and that's why preachers continue to preach the same thing over and over to make sure that hearers know what it means to live by faith, not by hope.

God has a prize for you to possess.

Dr. Tony Evans, in his book, *America's Only Hope: Impacting Society in the '90s* (Moody Publishers, 1993), tells the story of a champion chess player who is on vacation. Being the world champion, he goes to an art gallery and began to survey all the structures and the paintings on the wall, just enjoying himself. He sees a painting that captivates him. The painting is a chess board. He notices the pieces are already at certain locations on the board. Then he notices the devil on one side of the picture shouting, having a good time, in jubilation. He sees a young person on the other side, sweat pouring down his face. Fear was on his face, and then he saw the title of the painting—*Checkmate*. The devil was claiming the soul of the young man. The champion chess player was intrigued as he began to look at the position of all the board pieces. He put his champion chess stare on it and kept searching. Suddenly, he smiled and looked at the young man. There was good news! There was one more move on the chessboard—it was the young man's move.

> *Never forget that the devil is a liar and a thief, but God has come that you can have life and have it more abundantly.*

Never forget that the devil is a liar and a thief, but God has come that you can have life and have it more abundantly. The devil thought he had Jesus when Jesus came down through forty-two generations. The devil had already captivated by death—Adam, Abraham, Noah, all the prophets. He had everybody captivated, locked up by death. Then came a man named Jesus, who had come down through forty-two generations, walked the dusty roads of Palestine, healed the sick, gave sight to the blind, fed thousands—then they marched Him up a hill called Calvary. They put nails in His hands and in His feet, and a crown of thorns on His head. I can see the devil liking that picture saying, "I got Him now!" He who had no sin died on a cross between two thieves. He became sin on earth. Not only did He die physically, not only did He give His life physically, He also died spiritually, saying, "My God, My God, why hast Thou forsaken me?" Why did He say this? He had taken in all humanity's sins on Him.

Psalm 22 ends with, "It is finished," and the Bible says Jesus spoke those words and descended into hell. I can see the devil right now and all his lunatic angels saying, "Somebody just came who's breaking down all our doors," and strongholds came down on Satan's throne. Jesus goes to the throne. The devil said, Jesus, what are you doing here? You must be dead."

"Yes, I did die on the cross."

"Jesus, what you doing here? You got to have sin."

"I took all the sins of the world." Then Jesus said, "Give me those keys." Jesus took the keys from the devil. Three days later His spirit joined back with His body, and He went to the room where His disciples were hiding. According to John 20, Jesus walked in the room and said, "Peace be unto you" (v. 19). Suddenly, the disciples recognized it was Jesus. He bid them peace two times (vv. 19, 21) and calmed their hearts. Then He did what He came to do. He breathed the Holy Spirit on them (v. 22). Everything Jesus had gone through was for that purpose. He came to take humanity back to Genesis chapters one and two and to give us back our dominion and control of this earth.

Jesus said, "All authority is given to me in heaven and on earth (see Matthew 28:18), and because I have all the authority, I am giving it to you to go make disciples. Use my name and the keys I have taught you to bind up things on earth and to loose things on earth." He did this because the victory is already won. The devil only tries to make you think he is ruling by bluffing. The devil has no power but he is still faking people out because they think he does.

God wants you on earth as long as He can have you here so you can do His will. That's why the Bible tells us, "Therefore, I beseech you about the mercies of God, that you present your bodies as living sacrifice." God is saying that your spirit needs an earthly house, and your body is it. Therefore, take care of your body as best as you can because your spirit must remain in it. When the body deteriorates, you will die. To be absent from the body is then to be present with the Lord (2 Corinthians 5:8).

Then, when you get to heaven, you're going to get a prize. The Master will look to you and say "You ran your race with a purpose. You obeyed me. You had to deal with some challenges, some heartaches and pain. You recognized you had the authority and the power. You've been faithful over a few things (Matthew 25:21), now I'll make you ruler over many things. Enter the Kingdom with joy."

That's what God is saying to us. Our prize is for the Master to look at us and say well done, because you have been faithful.

About the Author

"The ultimate measure of a man is not where he stands in moments of comfort and convenience, but where he stands at times of challenge and controversy. Nothing worthwhile is easy. Your ability to overcome unfavorable situations will provide you with time to demonstrate your true strength and determination for success. Always set your standards high, your greatest achievements lie within the infinite feats you achieve in your life."

~Martin Luther King Jr.

Dr. Kenneth Bernard Weathersby is a man of God with a foundation of faith and family with a heart to uplift the name of Jesus. He has dedicated more than forty years in pastoral and denominational ministry. He manifests the ultimate measure of a man and has become a respected trailblazer, having been recognized internationally as a "friend of pastors" and as a strategist in church planting, a specialist in church growth and development, and a mobilizer of African-American and ethnic ministry partnerships.

About the Author

He was appointed the first African-American endowed chair in church planting at New Orleans Baptist Theological Seminary, and strategist and ministry leader at the Tennessee Baptist Mission Board and the North American Mission Board.

Having retired as the first African-American vice-president of convention advancement with the Southern Baptist Convention, Executive Committee, Dr. Weathersby continues to plant seeds under whose shade he may never sit through consultation and training among pastors and ministry leaders across the nation and the world.

www.ingramcontent.com/pod-product-compliance
Lightning Source LLC
Chambersburg PA
CBHW031426290426
44110CB00011B/547